3/12

the Feminine Face *of* Christianity

D1309521

the Feminine Face *of* Christianity

Margaret Starbird

Quest Books
Theosophical Publishing House

Wheaton, Illinois ♦ Chennai (Madras), India

Quest Books
are published by
The Theosophical Society in America
Wheaton, Illinois 60189-0270,
a worldwide, not-for-profit, membership
organization promoting fellowship
among all peoples of the world,
encouraging the study of religion,
philosophy, and science,
and facilitating spiritual growth
and healing.

Today humanity is on the verge of
becoming, for the first time in its history,
a global community. The only question
is what kind of community it will be.
Quest Books strives to fulfill the purpose
of the Theosophical Society to act as a
leavening; to introduce into humanity a
large mindedness, a freedom from bias,
an understanding of the values of the
East and West; and to point the way to
human development as a means of
service, both for the individual and for
the whole of humankind.

For more information about Quest
Books, visit www.questbooks.net.
For more information about the
Theosophical Society, visit
www.theosophical.org,
or contact Olcott@theosmail.net,
or (630) 668-1571.

Copyright © 2003 Godsfield Press
Text copyright © 2003 Margaret Starbird

First Quest Edition 2003
Copublished with Godsfield Press 2003

The Theosophical Publishing House
P.O. Box 270
Wheaton, Illinois 60189-0270

Designed and produced for Godsfield Press by
The Bridgewater Book Company

Picture research by Lynda Marshall

Library of Congress Cataloging-in-Publication Data
Starbird, Margaret
The feminine face of Christianity / Margaret Starbird.—1st Quest ed.
p. cm.
Includes bibliographical references and index.
ISBN 0-8356-0827-1
1. Christian women—Biography.   2. Women in Christianity.
I. Title.
BR1713 .S73 2003
270'.082—dc21
                                                        2002031616

Printed and bound in China

1   2   3   4   5   6   7   8   9   10

CONTENTS

Christianity Today

oised at the dawn of its third millennium, Christianity is the faith of more than two billion people spread across every continent on the globe. The sheer diversity of the responses to the Christian "faith of our fathers" is a powerful testimony to the ongoing relevance of the Gospels and the message of Jesus Christ. But institutional Christianity is under intense scrutiny; its history and core values are being examined by scholars and by faithful practitioners, as well as by people of other faiths. Issues include the witness of the earliest Christians and the doctrines promulgated by Christian institutions. What was the experience of the earliest followers of Jesus Christ that led to their enthusiastic preaching of the Good News and

Christian mission workers are the living embodiment of the Gospel message of love and compassion, working in a hospital in Rwanda, with young victims of civil war.

the *kerygma*, or "proclamation," of the risen Lord? What were the unique teachings of the Jewish "Rabbi Yesh" that attracted such loyal followers? What are the fundamental values of Christianity and how do they affect women? And, in particular, why do large numbers of women embrace this faith so passionately, "giving of their substance," as did the earliest female followers of Jesus mentioned in the Gospels?

Our quest here is to recover the experience—the faces and voices—of women throughout the centuries who have been among the most ardent and devoted disciples of Jesus. Who were these women? What did they believe? What do Mary Magdalene, Catherine of Siena, Joan of Arc, and Mother Teresa have in common, and what is their relevance for women who walk the Christian journey today? This book will explore these tenets of Christianity and unveil the face of the Divine Feminine as she finds expression in the preeminent faith of Western civilization, particularly in the New Testament Scriptures, in various Marian revelations, prayers, and practices, and in the lives of numerous Christians who have walked in the Light of Christ.

Wonderful archetypes of the Sacred Feminine are found in the mythology surrounding the charismatic figure of Jesus: Mother, Bride, Holy Sophia, and the Grail provide rich associations with the Divine. In addition to its broader themes, we will here examine some of Christianity's powerful feminine symbols and archetypes: the dove, the grail-chalice, the rose, the tower, the Holy City, the enclosed garden, the streams of living water—symbols found in the art, architecture, and literature of the Christian tradition. Our journey into these areas is enhanced by numerous illustrations—drawings and paintings representing various aspects of the Sacred Feminine found in Christianity. Also included are numerous suggestions for spiritual practice. Prayers, poems, liturgies, and meditations—both traditional and modern—are offered at the end of each chapter, in the hope that they may provide manna for the spiritual journey and encourage the pilgrim to experience more fully the feminine aspects of Christianity.

In addition, we will examine fundamental tenets of the Christian faith that are feminine in nature. The most fundamental "feminine" tenet of Christianity is the immanence of the Divine implicit in the doctrine of the Incarnation. God is not purely transcendent, but becomes flesh in the man Jesus, partaking of the human condition. The Incarnation represents the intrinsic partnership of flesh and spirit, and the "reign of God" is already among us and even now "in our midst." Christianity manifests other strongly feminine elements: radical inclusiveness and equality, compassion, reconciliation, and the healing of crippled bodies, broken hearts, and bitter relationships. Those who have "ears to hear" are called to do what Jesus did: to minister to the lowly and sorrowful, to feed the hungry, to bring justice to the oppressed. The blind see and the deaf hear. Prisoners are set free and the Good News of the resurrection into eternal life is made available to all, regardless of rank or social position.

Christianity is a powerful equalizer. Its fertile seeds, planted in the hills of Judea, gradually spread throughout the Roman Empire and eventually from Europe to the Western Hemisphere. The Gospel teachings have helped to produce an abundant harvest of democracy, freedom, and social justice that continues to spread across the planet. The words of Jesus are also distinctly pacifist. His followers are exhorted to love and pray for their enemies, wishing them well and forgiving those who have offended them.

A significant theme permeating the Gospels is the motif of the Bridegroom, a characterization derived from the prophets who presented God as the eternal and faithful Bridegroom and Israel as his chosen Bride. This sacred partnership of God and humanity, divinity and flesh, "Bridegroom" and "Bride" is found at the very heart of the Christian message. Close examination of the canonical Gospels strongly suggests that Jesus was widely recognized as the "Bridegroom of Israel" and that he was acutely conscious of this role. Those who had "ears to hear" recognized the voice of the Bridegroom—the anointed Messiah of his people.

But it was not a priest of the Temple who anointed Jesus as the Messiah. We must also examine the Sacred Marriage indigenous to Christianity and its deep connection with the surprising story of the anointing of Jesus by a woman—a story so powerful that it appears in all four canonical Gospels. We wish to examine the response of later generations to Christ, the eternal Bridegroom, following the example of the contemplative provided by Mary, the sister of Lazarus, who sat at the feet of Jesus and on one memorable occasion anointed them with her tears and wiped them with her hair (John 12). For two millennia spiritual seekers have followed her way of the heart to union with the Beloved.

Devotion to the Virgin Mary has played an extraordinary role in the spirituality of many Christians. Christians honor the "Great Mother," who provides a model for perfect faith, perfect trust, and perfect obedience. Sublime medieval temples celebrate her role as Queen of Heaven. Although she speaks only a few words in the Gospels, Mary's influence among Christians is unparalleled, and the power of her intercession is legendary. Christians saw in the "Mother of God" the face of the Divine Feminine, celebrating her holy motherhood while honoring her perpetual virginity. She was "mediatrix" of all grace and blessing, and pilgrims seek her shrines—including those of the enigmatic Black Virgin prevalent in southern Europe—in supplication for her favors and intercession.

The powerful witness of the women who actually walked with Jesus quietly fed generations of faithful women who heard the Gospel. *The Feminine Face of Christianity* looks at stories of numerous faith-filled Christian women—both historical and contemporary—who embraced the example of the biblical women who knew the "Rabbi Yesh" who walked the dusty roads of Palestine in sandals. Martyrs, mystics, scholars, and activists; virgins, wives, and mothers—countless women manifest the great themes of Christianity: the presence of the Spirit indwelling our "earthen vessels," the sanctity of human life, and the constant and challenging quest for peace and social justice. Their stories inspire us to embody the wisdom, grace, and trust so evident in their example.

While traditions later derived from Paul's Epistles kept women silent in the pews of Christian churches, Christ's own words and example have persistently worked to set them free. Ongoing research is uncovering the leadership roles of women in the first generations of Christians. We will here examine the gradual loosening of the shackles of women from the early silence imposed on them through the centuries, culminating with the experience of contemporary women of faith who continue to walk in intimate communion with the Lord. Only now—in the early light of the third Christian millennium—are we able to reclaim the original clarion call of Jesus for full equality, freedom, and justice for all.

Clement of Alexandria (c. 150–215), one of the most highly educated of the early Church fathers, described Christianity as the "New Song" that tunes the discord of the world into a great harmony. He seems to have envisioned a universal symphony evolving from the teachings of Christ, an ecstatic harmony of melodies emerging from the heart of the Christian community and rising to fill the cosmos. Clement's vision has yet to reach its fulfillment, in part because, for centuries, the voices of women were silenced by the institutional hierarchy. The orthodox or "straight thinkers" gradually rooted out diverse teachings and interpretations and concretized the new religion under strict guidelines: one Lord, one faith, one bishop, one creed. Everyone was to sing the same tune, in the same key. Under the aegis of the mighty Roman eagle, the people of the fourth-century empire became Christians, but diversity was repressed in favor of conformity to carefully formulated and concretized doctrine—and eventually codified into a formidable body of canon law.

The gradual "unveiling" of women in Christian nations has been a powerful catalyst for social change, especially since the nineteenth century and beyond, continuing toward a powerful crescendo.

Women's voices are now raised not only in support of gender equality, but in pleas for protection of the environment and in supplication for peace and harmony among all peoples—for the sake of the children of the entire planet. Nuns and lay women of all denominations are now being heard, their voices becoming part of the chorus reaching toward a crescendo never before heard on earth. The New Song is the wedding song of the Lamb and his Bride—the "New Jerusalem."

Watching televised reports in November 2001 showing women of Kabul throwing off their bourkas was an intensely spiritual event. We stand at the threshold of the new millennium and witness the "unveiling" of the feminine worldwide. In the Apocalypse of John (the Book of Revelation), the "Bride" representing the purified and chastened Church is arrayed in her wedding garments to be joined in marriage with the eternal Bridegroom, Jesus. The Church of which we speak is not a building. It is a living body, the community of faith-filled Christians. An obscure line found deep in the document that emerged from the Second Vatican Council suggested that the bishops of the Church should listen to the people, for the Spirit of God rests in the people. It is the people who are the "Bride," and at the dawn of the new millennium, it is the voice of the people that is being heard at last: "There shall yet be heard the cry of joy, the cry of gladness, the voice of the Bridegroom, the voice of the Bride" (Jer. 33.10–11). In this book, we attempt to lift the veil from the face to reveal that feminine face of Christianity—the Bride of Christ.

CHAPTER ONE

WOMEN WHO WALKED WITH JESUS

His mother, his sister,
and his companion were each a Mary.

(THE GNOSTIC GOSPEL OF PHILIP, FROM THE NAG HAMMADI LIBRARY[1])

Women who Walked with Jesus

After two thousand years the charismatic personality of Jesus Christ continues to fascinate and appeal to a broad spectrum of people—passionate believers and casual observers alike. This fascination with Jesus has continued since the very beginning of his ministry in hamlets of the remote Roman province of Judea, where people crowded to see him and to hear his teachings, to touch his robe, and to beg for his healing touch: "Rabbi, my servant is ill. But only say the word, and he shall be healed" (Luke 7.7).

What drew people to Jesus? What persuaded his disciples to abandon comfortable, conventional lifestyles to follow him, even into deprivation and martyrdom? And why were many of his most ardent and faithful devotees women from the upper ranks of society—women from households throughout the pagan Roman Empire as well as women of Jewish heritage? Stories told of Jesus in an oral tradition and later recorded in the canonical Gospels of Matthew, Mark, Luke, and John provide us with clues.

Given the milieu in which he lived, Jesus was unique, even revolutionary. He waived the double standards so widespread in first-century Judaism and in the Roman Empire. In fact, one might even claim that Jesus was a radical egalitarian!

This young woman in Haiti has just received the holy sacrament of Baptism, and is committing her life to living the message of the Gospels.

He expected the same high standards of behavior from each person, male or female, based on the ancient commandments of Judaism. To the commandment in Deuteronomy, "Love the Lord your God with your whole heart and with your whole soul and with your whole strength," Jesus adds "and love your neighbor as yourself" (Mark 12.29–31). He upholds the Ten Commandments revealed to Moses, proclaiming that he came, not to destroy the Law, but to fulfill it.

But clearly Jesus believed strongly in the spirit of the law behind the letter. When a self-righteous crowd of men confronted Jesus with a woman caught in the act of adultery, Jesus did not uphold the law of Israel, which required that the woman be stoned to death. Instead he turned the tables on the accusers: "Let whoever is without sin cast the first stone" (John 8.7). One at a time, the men dropped their stones and hurried away. Implicit in this passage is the question, "Where is the man who was caught with this adulterous woman? It takes two to commit adultery." Jesus came to challenge inequalities with his new "Way"—the way of reconciliation, forgiveness, and forbearance. No wonder the marginalized, the oppressed, and the women of Judea flocked in great numbers to hear him teach.

Surprising attitudes of tolerance and inclusiveness are attributed to Jesus, reflected in his recorded teachings: "Judge not, that ye be not judged" (Matt. 7.1). According to testimony found in the Gospels, forgiveness should be extended not just seven times, but seventy times seven! "If a man . . . takes your tunic, give him your cloak as well"

An ancient Byzantine mosaic from the Church of the Hagia Sophia in the former Constantinople shows Mary seated in majesty holding in the Divine Child on her lap.

(Matt. 5.40). "Love your enemies and do good unto them!" (Matt. 5.44). Often Jesus indicted the proud and self-righteous elite, dressed in their finery, praying aloud and giving alms conspicuously so that they would be honored for their generosity: "It is easier for a camel to pass through the eye of a needle than for a wealthy person to enter God's kingdom" (Mark 10.25). The recorded teachings of Jesus were nothing short of revolutionary for his time. In fact, the more outrageous and radical the statement attributed to him, according to some modern Bible scholars, the more likely that it is an authentic saying of Jesus!

Jesus and Women in the Gospels

Included in the four Gospels of the official canon are stories about Jesus' compassion for women. Many were healed by his touch. The twelve-year-old daughter of the official Jairus was raised from the dead, and a woman with the flux who secretly touched his robe was healed immediately and unconditionally. "Your faith has saved you," was the disclaimer of Jesus when those whom he cured tried to thank him. He did not claim to heal, but felt himself to be a channel for healing. The daughter of a Canaanite woman was healed of demonic possession even though she was not one of the Children of Israel; and another woman, a cripple for eighteen years, was cured on the Sabbath. The inclusive attitude of Jesus permeates the Scriptures. A scorned Samaritan is styled in the Gospel parable as the kind and generous "neighbor" who saves the life of the Jew injured by thieves and left for dead, ignored by his own countrymen—including a priest. Jesus reserves some of his harshest indictments for priests, whom he chastises for hypocrisy, in the vein of the Hebrew prophet Ezekiel who repudiates the priests of the Temple as "shepherds who shepherd themselves instead of the sheep" (Ezek. 34). Like Yahweh, who promises to shepherd the sheep himself, Jesus calls himself "the Good Shepherd" whose sheep hear his voice. Jesus redefines ethics with respect to the Law, delving beneath the surface to examine the hypocrisy and hardness of heart—"cardiosclerosis"—that motivate selfish human behavior.

In the first century, a Jewish woman could not legally bear witness in court, and yet, Jesus entrusted to women his most profound revelations. In John's Gospel, we read that Jesus conversed with the Samaritan woman at the well, revealing himself to her as the long-awaited Messiah of Israel. The first disciple to encounter him after his resurrection was also a woman—the Mary called "the Magdalene"—whom Jesus instructed to go tell his brothers what she had seen. Women also appear in the Gospel parables in other very sympathetic scenarios. A poor widow quietly places two tiny coins in the alms box and wins praise from Jesus as an example of great generosity, because she "gave from her want."

Whoever welcomes one child such as this for my sake, welcomes me.
(MARK 9.37)

Even more surprising are incidents when Jesus compares God to a woman. Like the good shepherd who seeks for his one lost sheep, a widow lights a lamp and sweeps her entire house looking for a tiny lost coin, and then invites her neighbors in to rejoice with her when the coin is found. According to another of his teachings, the kingdom of God is like a woman who took a tiny bit of yeast and leavened the entire dough. These homely little parables illustrate the value of women in the eyes of Jesus. The women who heard the Gospel must have been deeply touched by the compassion of Jesus and his interest in the details of their lives. They still are!

A scene that portrays the three Marys (the Virgin Mary, her sister, and the Magdalene) mourning the crucified Christ before the ramparts of Jerusalem.

The Family from Bethany

Two women are especially supportive of Jesus, who often brought his entourage of friends to their home in Bethany. Scripture states unequivocally that Jesus loved these women—Martha and Mary—and their brother Lazarus, whom he raised from the dead (John 11). He often stayed as a guest at their house, conversing with them and sharing meals. In a story recorded in the Gospel of Luke, Mary chose to sit at the feet of Jesus, drinking in every word he spoke, while Martha was busy arranging for their meal. Finally, Martha complained to Jesus that Mary was not helping with the preparations, but Jesus defended the quiet sister, explaining that she had "chosen the better part." Based on this passage, Mary became the model for orders of contemplative nuns in later generations, sitting at the feet of the Savior and listening for his consoling and enlightening Word spoken directly to the attentive heart.

All that you ask for in prayer, believe that you shall receive it and it shall be yours.

(MARK 11.24)

It is this same Mary who in John's Gospel anointed Jesus and wiped her tears from his feet with her hair, an amazingly powerful story of passionate devotion to the Beloved. Rather than sell her expensive unguent as the disciples suggested, Jesus suggests that she keep the fragrant perfume for the day of his burial. From this passage, the Mary who anointed Christ at the banquet at Bethany was later conflated with the Mary called "the Magdalene," who went at dawn on Easter morning to the tomb to anoint the body of the crucified Christ for burial.

Many women followed Jesus, ministering to him and supporting his work with their personal wealth. Among these were Susannah and Joanna, the wife of Herod's steward Chuza. The most important of the women who accompanied him on his journey through the dusty villages of Galilee and Judah was Mary Magdalene, who, it is claimed, was cured of possession by seven demons, a frequent metaphor explaining mental illness such as depression or epilepsy. On seven of the eight lists naming the women who walked with Jesus, this Mary is mentioned first, while Mary, the mother of Jesus, is mentioned first only once. What did the earliest Christians know and believe about this woman called "the Magdalene" that persuaded them to designate her as "first lady" in their earliest stories and sacred texts?

The Blessed Virgin Mary

Of course, the archetype of the "Great Mother" is traditionally borne by the Blessed Virgin. Mary, the mother of Jesus, receives recognition in the nativity narratives of Matthew's and Luke's Gospels. In Luke's version, she was approached by the angel Gabriel who announced that she would conceive a son of the "Most High" and would name him Jesus. Birth mythologies of gods in the ancient world often involved a virgin mother who gave birth to a divine child under miraculous circumstances, frequently after an encounter with a god. This mythologizing was a way of showing that the child was specially chosen and charismatic—a gift from the gods. In the Greek pantheon, Maia was the virgin mother of Hermes, while Zeus miraculously gave birth to Athena from his own forehead and impregnated Leda in his guise of a swan. Other gods claimed in mythology to have been born of virgin mothers include Dionysus, Attis, Adonis, and Mithras, all of whom have strong "savior" attributes remarkably similar to those claimed for Jesus Christ. In the case of Jesus, conception was "by the Holy Spirit," which overshadowed the *alma*. In Hebrew, this word meant simply "a young woman"—Mary of Nazareth—and was mistranslated in Greek as *parthenon*, "an unmarried virgin."

In Luke's Gospel, shepherds tending their sheep follow the star over Bethlehem to find the baby Jesus wrapped in swaddling clothes and lying in a manger. In Matthew's story, magi-astrologers from the East attend the newborn baby. Bearing precious gifts of gold, frankincense, and myrrh, they travel to pay homage to the Divine Child whose birth is heralded by the star. Matthew's Gospel reports the flight of the Holy Family into Egypt to avoid the massacre of the infants by King Herod, while Luke's reports the circumcision and presentation of Jesus in the Temple on the eighth day after his birth, and the return visit when his worried parents find the twelve-year-old Jesus teaching the elders in the Temple. The stories in these two birth narratives were written independently of one another and cannot be traced to any earlier source. Both Matthew and Luke provide genealogies of Jesus stemming back to King David. Each claims to be the male line from David to Jesus

through Joseph the carpenter, but the names on the two accounts differ. Clearly these writers did not know one another's work. Their birth narratives have very few similarities, but each evangelist attempts in his own way to express the very special origins of the Christ Child—God's chosen and anointed, the heir of David.

Christian Art

Familiar themes of these Gospel stories occur often in Christian art. The archetype of the Virgin receiving the message of the angel was a very popular theme for medieval artists. A dove representing the Holy Spirit often accompanies the archangel Gabriel. The Virgin is typically young and demure, often grasping a white Madonna lily. Her forearms are occasionally crossed over her breast in a pose of sweet surrender to the will and word of God. In several medieval paintings, the "Alma Mary" is presented with a tiny baby in swaddling clothes entering her ear at the moment of conception. The symbolic content of these paintings expresses the belief that Mary, the prototype of every Christian, receives the Word of God through her ear; the result of this encounter is that the Word is made flesh in her. All Christians are like the Virgin Mary. They hear the Word of God and receive it into the fertile ground of their hearts, where it takes root and permeates their lives as Christians. And "the Word becomes flesh"—in them! In this way a Christian becomes the "hands and feet of God."

This same fundamental understanding also underlies the Church's teaching of the Holy

In this archetypal image of mother and child, normally depicted in Christian icons of the Blessed Virgin and the Christ Child, the Egyptian goddess Isis suckles her son Horus, the fruit of her posthumous union with the god Osiris.

arms. These artifacts are reminiscent of ancient renderings of the Egyptian goddess Isis seated with her son Horus on her lap, the mother and child archetype ubiquitous in human experience. More unusual is the occasional painting showing the baby Jesus *in utero*, an ancient representation of the sacred opposites found in the Divine: male and female, old and young. Icons of the Holy Mother and her child are honored in shrines worldwide and are the objects of great devotion and pilgrimage in many regions.

Eucharist, another expression of the intimate union of the Divine incarnate—becoming flesh—in the faithful. Paul states in his First Epistle to the Corinthians that the body is a temple of the Holy Spirit. The treasure we hold is not of gold; it is the Christ "in earthen vessels"! All this is revealed visually in paintings of the Virgin with the Christ Child *in utero*, or approaching her ear. The paintings are not so naïve as they first appear.

The nativity of Jesus is a frequent subject for painters, but even more prevalent are pictures and sculptures of the Madonna holding Jesus in her

In later passages of the synoptic Gospels, the mother of Jesus receives very little attention until the Crucifixion of her son. When she arrives with the brothers of Jesus and wishes to speak with him, Jesus is reported to have asked, "Who are my mother and brothers? Those who do the will of the Father are my mother and brothers and sisters." When Jesus visited Nazareth, villagers tried to chase him out of town, and his own relatives attempted to seize him because they thought he was out of his mind (Mark 3). But Mary reappears at Golgotha where she suffers at the foot of her son's cross, supported by the other women in the group. Apparently the male disciples were in hiding; only the women and the "Beloved Disciple" attended the Crucifixion.

Paintings and sculptures of the Blessed Virgin receiving the body of her son when he is taken from the cross are archetypal renderings of the "sorrowful mother." In just the same way, Isis holds the mutilated body of her husband Osiris, conceiving their child Horus posthumously according to their myth. In Christianity's mythology, the archetypes of mother and bride are separated; in Western art, it is often the Virgin Mary who cradles the head while Mary Magdalene bends tenderly over the feet of Jesus at the Deposition, often with her hair touching his feet—recalling the anointing scene in the Gospels. Other women accompany the two Marys at the cross and at the tomb, but the Magdalene and the mother of Jesus are both specifically mentioned in the Gospel narratives of the Crucifixion while the male disciples are significantly absent from the scene.

Mary Magdalene in Art

It was the Magdalene who first came to the tomb at dawn on Easter morning and found it empty (John 20). And it was she who encountered the risen Lord and tried to embrace him. "Do not cling to me," he admonished her, "but go tell my brothers . . ." She was the first witness of the Resurrection, tasked with reporting the "Good News" to the male apostles. But since Jewish women in the first century were not considered by law to be valid witnesses, she was not believed. This tender scene in the garden is a favorite of Christian artists.

The encounter of Mary Magdalene and Christ near the tomb in the garden is powerfully reminiscent of the ancient ritual of the *hieros gamos* cult—the "Sacred Marriage." Liturgical rites of the "Sacrificed Bridegroom" from ancient fertility cults were widely practiced in the Near East for several millennia. Undoubtedly the people of the Roman Empire were familiar with these rites and recognized the liturgical sequence that began with the anointing of Jesus by Mary, the sister of Lazarus (John 12.1–2). The anointing of Jesus is one of only four stories that occur in each of the canonical Gospels, attesting to its prominence in the community of Christians who retained the oral tradition surrounding the life and ministry of Jesus. (The three other stories are the Baptism of Jesus by John in the River Jordan, the multiplication of the loaves and the fishes, and the Crucifixion.) The anointing by the woman must have been "told and retold in memory of her" for a special reason: indeed, it is the key to the "sacred union" at the heart of the Gospels!

In various ancient traditions, the liturgical sequence of the "sacrificed Bridegroom" began with the king's nuptials: he was anointed by the Bride in a solemn rite prefiguring the anointing of the male during the marital act, which took place in the private seclusion of the bridal chamber after the public ritual anointing of the king. When the royal couple later reemerged after consummating their nuptials, their union was celebrated

> *Many who are first will be last, and the last will be first.*
> (MARK 10.31)

Sister, we know that the Savior loved you more than the rest of women.
(PETER IN THE GNOSTIC "GOSPEL OF MARY"[2])

throughout the city, and their joy and delight spread out into the realm and encouraged the fertility of its crops and herds. Later in the liturgical year, the Bridegroom was ritually mutilated, sacrificed, and laid in a tomb. On the third day, in some of these myths, his bereaved widow came with her women to mourn at his tomb and found him resurrected in the garden. Such similar elements to the Gospel story seem to be typical in the cults of ancient god/goddess couples: Dumuzi and Inanna; Tammuz and Ishtar; Attis and Cybele; Venus and Adonis; Osiris and Isis. In Christianity, "new wine" is being poured into new vessels: Christ and Mary Magdalene together incarnate the ancient mythology of the Bridegroom King and his Bride, who symbolically represents her entire nation—the "Daughter of Sion." Hippolytus of Rome and several other early exegetes of Christian Scripture readily recognized the Mary called "the Magdalene" as the archetype of the Church community (*ekklesia*) whom Paul calls the Bride whom Christ loved so much, he gave his life for her (Eph. 5.25).

In Western art, Mary Magdalene is almost invariably carrying her alabaster jar of precious nard, a fragrant and expensive perfume made from an exotic plant that is native to the slopes of the Himalayas. Very early Church tradition identified her with the Mary who anointed Jesus at the banquet at Bethany, the sister of Lazarus and Martha. Occasionally in paintings she is holding a book, the symbol of "Holy Wisdom," the *Sophia*. Now and then, she is pictured with a skull, a reminder of the human condition and the transitory nature of all flesh, but also of the pall of death hovering over the hill of Golgotha, the "Place of the Skull" where Jesus was crucified. In a famous painting by George de la Tour, the Magdalene has a large

This sixteenth-century fresco of Mary Magdalene by Gianfrancesco da Tolmezzo shows her carrying her alabaster jar of ointment.

irregular pearl on the table near her—the "pearl of great price" that is a metaphor for the kingdom of God. In this remarkable painting, *The Magdalene with the Twin Flames*, her mirror reflects the light of her candle, as her life reflects the light and love of her Beloved, and as the moon reflects the light of the sun, and as the Divine Feminine, the Sophia, is the reflection or mirror of God's Wisdom.

Often in medieval paintings, Mary Magdalene is robed in green, a color sacred also to Isis and symbolic of fertility and renewal. At other times, she is clothed in cloth of gold brocade, the fabric worn by the Bride of the Messiah in the biblical "Song of a Royal Wedding":

> All glorious is the king's
> daughter as she enters,
> her raiment threaded with gold;
> in embroidered apparel
> she is led to the king . . .
> Ps. 45.13–14

Very often in art, Mary Magdalene wears a crimson or scarlet cloak, pointedly referring to her passionate carnal nature. But the Gospels never call her a prostitute. This spurious epithet was probably derived from her anointing of the Messiah. In pagan liturgical rites associated with the Sacrificed Bridegroom, the anointing of the Sacred King was done by a *hierodule*, or "consecrated woman," a word often translated (with severely negative connotations) as "sacred prostitute." The more ancient nuptial ritual associated with the anointing was evidently suppressed in the Christian tradition, possibly to protect the bereaved widow of Jesus from the threatening scrutiny of Roman authorities.

French Legends of the Holy Grail

French legend states that Mary Magdalene and her family and friends, who were fleeing early persecutions of Christians, arrived safely on the Mediterranean coast of France near the town now called Saintes-Maries-de-la-Mer. It is claimed that she brought with her the Holy Grail, a relic treasured because it once held the blood of Christ. Several medieval paintings depict Joseph of Arimathea holding up the chalice from which Jesus had drunk at the Last Supper. In this sacred vessel, according to legend, Joseph caught the blood flowing from the wounded side of Jesus on the cross. These paintings illustrate the literal explanation for the Grail legends—the chalice that once contained the blood of Christ. An esoteric explanation, branded heretical, suggests that the Magdalene herself was the sacred vessel of the *sangraal* (or *sangreal*) of French legend, which can be read *sang raal* (literally, the "blood royal"). One does not carry the "blood royal" in a jar with a lid. In the latter case, the symbolism of the Grail legends reveals that the wounded Fisher-King and his wasteland realm are healed, not by a chalice, but by the restoration of the archetypal "lost Bride" of the Christian tradition embodied in Mary Magdalene. This is the basis for the "heresy of the Holy Grail" that surfaced during the Middle Ages and appears to have been the faith of the alternative Christian medieval "Church of Love."

Festival of Saint Sarah and the Three Marys

Surviving in the town of Saintes-Maries-de-la-Mer is the story of Saint Sarah the Egyptian, an adolescent child who accompanied the three Marys on their journey into exile. This young girl does not appear in the Bible, but the statue of the black Saint Sarah occupies the smoky crypt of the Basilica of Our Lady of the Sea in the village square. Every year, a festival is celebrated in honor of Saint Sarah and the three "Marys": Mary Magdalene, Mary Salome, and Mary "Jacobi," the mother of James, who traveled to this distant shore bringing the Grail and the Gospel. In a colorful folk festival celebrated from May 23–25, statues of the saints are taken from the church and paraded through the town and out to the rocky beach on the Mediterranean, to commemorate their arrival in western Europe in 42 C.E. in a boat with no oars. On May 24, a cortege of Gypsy men astride white horses of the Camargue and arrayed in traditional garb accompanies the statue of the dark Saint Sarah, the patron saint of Gypsies who were once believed, like her, to have come from Egypt. To the delight of thousands of townspeople and visitors gathered for the festival, the mounted escort stands in the sea, their horses prancing in the breaking waves of the rising tide, holding the statue of the little saint who traveled so far in the company of the first witnesses to the risen Christ.

The three Marys who walked with Jesus, who stood vigil at his cross and were first to visit his empty tomb, provide a model of faithful devotion to Christ, the Beloved. At the same time they echo the triple aspects of the Divine Feminine: maiden/sister, spouse/childbearer, and crone/wise woman. Often in paintings of the Crucifixion and deposition of the body of Jesus, the women can be identified at the foot of the cross, or embracing the corpse, and again at the tomb on Easter morning. They are called *myrrhophores*, "bearers of bitter perfume for anointing the dead," a duty performed by female members of the family of the deceased.

The celebration of the three Marys in the little French town that honors their memory also echoes a recently discovered text found in 1945 near the village of Nag Hammadi in Egypt. The Gnostic Gospel of Philip states that there were three Marys who walked with the Lord: "Mary his mother and her sister and Magdalene, the one who was called his companion." At the dawn of this new millennium, Mary Magdalene emerges from these third-century texts with renewed power and influence—"the one whom Jesus loved more than all the disciples." Tradition credits the Apostle Philip with evangelizing France, and it is exactly here that the influence of the hidden gospel that bears his name is the strongest, reflected in the ubiquitous presence of Mary Magdalene. Her chapels, grottos, springs, and vineyards bear witness to the high honor in which she was held from the very earliest days of Christianity. Her statues grace alcoves of medieval churches while supplicants for her compassionate intercession light votive candles at her feet. Meadows of southern France are filled with her fragrant perfume, and scarlet poppies spring from the very ground where, according to legend, her feet trod.

PRACTICE:
PRAYER–STOLE MEDITATION

To get in closer touch with the loving energy of the Blessed Mother or Mary Magdalene, select or create a prayer stole. Perhaps you will choose an elegant one—of velvet, silk, or brocade—or a length of fabric in beautiful colors. Or, if you prefer, a simple dark blue, dark red, or white stole is appropriate. In front of a mirror, drape your stole over your head and shoulders. Select a comfortable chair near the altar you have created or in a darkened room and light a candle. You may choose to put on some very unobtrusive background music (without lyrics), or use a special fragrance to help establish the mood. Sit very quietly, breathing peacefully, waiting expectantly for the "Lady" to be present to you. Soak in the gentle feminine energy that gradually surrounds and envelops you during this meditation. Try to allow fifteen or twenty minutes for this spiritual exercise. Take the time to record your impressions and any insights you receive in a journal kept for this special purpose.

Entering into a state of deep and prayerful meditation will enable you to connect in a much closer way with the powerful and loving energy of the Blessed Virgin Mary.

CHAPTER TWO

VIRGINS, MARTYRS, AND DESERT MOTHERS

Jesus said
Sell whatsoever thou hast and give to the poor . . .
and take up thy cross and follow me.

(LUKE 18.22)

Virgins, Martyrs, and Desert Mothers

Although the Gospel narrative records that Jesus himself was seen to eat and drink with his associates, enjoying banquets and celebrating the good things in life, a tradition of ascetic spiritual practice is associated with Christianity. Mystics, virgins, and martyrs seem to have been held in the highest esteem by medieval Christians. The themes of physical self-denial and mortification of the flesh appear to have derived from the experience of Christians in the generations that followed the Crucifixion, using Jesus' ultimate sacrifice on the cross as their model. Persecutions of Christian sectarians began almost immediately; one of the earliest recorded stories from the fledgling faith is the stoning of Stephen found in the New Testament Acts of the Apostles. And those who heeded the preaching of Paul were admonished to prepare for the "kingdom of God" that would soon overtake the world in a violent upheaval. They were encouraged to embrace the spiritual path with its corollary denial of the flesh, even to

remain unwed. Martyrs and virgins formed the first echelon of saints who received their eternal reward in heaven. In Revelation, the final book of the Christian Bible, they are found accompanying the Lamb and singing a "New Song" of praise to God.

Among early Christians, virgins and martyrs occupied positions of highest esteem. Peter is pictured here with a woman, possibly his daughter, Petronilla, who died a saint, a virgin, and a martyr.

Mysticism

Of course, not all of the early Christians were destined to be martyrs. Some cultivated the path of mysticism modeled in the Gospel narratives, which present Jesus as an itinerant mystic and prophet in the Jewish tradition. Immediately after his baptism by his cousin John the Baptist in the River Jordan, Jesus went into the desert beyond the Jordan where, according to Matthew's Gospel, he fasted for forty days and was tempted by the devil. During his ministry in the Roman province of Judea, Jesus often left the crowds and his disciples behind and sought the solitude of the hills in order to quietly pray. He was especially strong in advocating prayer done privately, and not using "vain repetitions as the pagans do," but he also provided a prayer for his followers to use when addressing "Abba," their loving parent in heaven. Two millennia later, this prayer is treasured still—the "Our Father" (*Pater Noster*) taught to every Christian child.

Many statements attributed to Jesus have a strong mystic element: "I and the Father are One," and "The words that I speak to you I do not speak on my own. The Father who dwells in me is doing his works. Believe me that I am in the Father and the Father is in me . . ." (John 14.10–11). This language is typical of the experience of mystics from every religious tradition who experience intimate oneness with the Divine Source. The essence of mysticism is the prayer of silence in the presence of the Divine, which is a distinctly passive and "feminine" stance, where the still mind and heart of the seeker await in quiet expectation the gentle touch of the Beloved.

In the Gospels, Jesus promises that he will be in continued communion with those who follow him: "Wherever two or three are gathered in my name, there am I in the midst of them" (Matt. 18.20). This invitation to remain united with him is reinforced in the Book of Revelation: "Behold, I stand at the door and knock. If anyone hears my voice and opens the door, I will come in and sup with him and he with me" (Rev. 3.20). Christians claim this intimate communion with their risen Savior, confident that the promise of Christ is meant for each believer.

PATER NOSTER

Our Father, who art in heaven,
hallowed be thy name.
Thy kingdom come, thy will be done,
on earth as it is in heaven.
Give us this day our daily bread.
And forgive us our debts
as we also forgive our debtors.
And lead us not into temptation
but deliver us from evil.

(MATT. 6.9–13)

One of the favorite metaphors of Christians is found in John's Gospel: "I am the vine, you are the branches. Whoever remains in me and I in him will bear much fruit"(John 15.5). And the promise to the universal Church is similar: "Behold, I am with you, even to the end of time" (Matt. 28.20). Early Christians took very literally these promises of Christ to be with them. How was this possible? Through the agency of the Holy Spirit, the *Paraclete,* or "traveling companion," who, Jesus promised, would come to comfort and abide with them: "I will send him to you . . . when he comes, the Spirit of truth, he will guide you to all truth." (John 16. 7–13). Passages like these from their Scriptures nourished and comforted the early Christians, who were marginalized and persecuted from the very earliest days of their community life. As the Lord remained with each individual, his abiding presence was felt also in the infant Christian community and later, as the Gospel spread to the far reaches of the Roman Empire, in the churches formed by converts to the new religion.

Fundamental to their faith was the idea that the Spirit of God found a dwelling place in each Christian: "Do you not know that you are the temple of God and that the Spirit of God dwells within you? . . . The Temple of God, which you are, is holy" (1 Cor. 3.16–17). Paul's epistles were written within a single generation of the Crucifixion. The Gospels were not yet written when Paul's words about Jesus were recorded and later copied and disseminated to the far-flung reaches of the empire. Official Christianity had two major literary sources: Paul's Epistles and the four

canonical Gospels, although numerous other texts soon embellished the earliest strata of stories about the life and ministry of Jesus. These other, often wildly imaginative and therefore less prestigious, legends and stories did not measure up to the strict standards for canonicity imposed by the Church fathers and are known as "apocrypha."

Persecutions in the Early Church

Paul, although he claimed to be an "apostle," had never known Jesus personally and had spent years persecuting Christians before his startling conversion experience. The Acts of the Apostles tells us that Paul was trying to destroy the Church and that he dragged Christian men and women out of their homes in order to have them imprisoned. He was planning to take his persecutions to Damascus, but on the journey a bright light flashed around him and he was thrown to the ground. Blinded by the intense light, he heard the voice of Jesus speaking to him: "Saul, Saul, why do you persecute me?" Saul was converted to the Way he had persecuted so severely. He changed his name from Saul to Paul and became an ardent missionary of Christianity. Paul's letters to various churches he helped to establish are remarkable in one respect: He never mentions any of the parables and teachings of Jesus that provide the material of the Gospels. His source is "personal revelation" from the Risen Lord and his own interpretation of Jesus as the fulfillment of Jewish prophecy concerning the expected Davidic Messiah.

The early Christians formed communities of house-churches, gathering quietly in people's homes to share their faith in Jesus, the good news of his Resurrection, and his ongoing presence with them, often sharing a simple Eucharist or thanksgiving meal of bread, fish, and wine. They held their property in common, welcoming the stranger and the dregs of society into their midst. On his missionary journeys throughout the Roman Empire, Paul stayed in the homes of Christians whose generosity to strangers and the poor became legendary, for they recognized Jesus present in each individual: "For I was hungry and you gave me food; I was thirsty, and you gave me drink; I was a stranger and you welcomed me, naked and you covered me" (Matt. 25.36).

Of all the teachings of Christianity, this is one of the most fundamentally "feminine" in nature: each individual is a *vas* or "vessel"—a sacred container indwelt by the Holy Spirit of God. The Virgin Mary is the prototypical Christian because, in her humble submission to the angel's proclamation, the Word of God becomes incarnate in her womb. She is the original sacred *vas* but all Christians are similarly called to be vessels of the incarnation. God becomes flesh in this way—Christians guided by the Holy Spirit within become the Divine's hands and feet; they know the mind and the heart of God. And what is true for the individual is also true for the whole community—the Church—as the vessel of the Spirit of God.

The followers of Jesus recoiled from the sexual permissiveness of the Hellenized culture of the Roman Empire. While Jesus often offered a loose interpretation of manmade rules in Judaism, waiving the strict Sabbath observance in order to cure a cripple and preventing an accused adulteress from being stoned, he was very strict about the sanctity of marriage.

The Sanctity of Marriage

Even though a man could easily obtain a divorce, both within Judaism and throughout the wider Roman Empire, Jesus does not approve of the practice. He said that Moses permitted divorce "because of your hardness of heart" (Matt. 19.8). From the beginning of creation, Jesus assured his listeners, "God made them male and female. For this reason a man shall leave his mother and father and cling to his wife, and the two shall be one flesh. . . . Therefore, what God has joined together, let no one separate" (Mark 10.6–9).

These authoritative statements attributed to Jesus himself powerfully reinforce the family unit as the fundamental unit in society—rooted in the committed lifelong union of loving partners. From this Bible passage alone, the status of women in the Christian community received almost revolutionary enhancement. Jewish law was very clear about the evils of fornication and adultery, but Jesus went one step further to protect the dignity and value of women: "But I say to you, if anyone lusts after a woman, he has already committed adultery in his heart" (Matt. 5.28). This man alone, the Rabbi Yesh, in his abbreviated lifetime, managed to plant the seeds that eventually revolutionized prevailing attitudes of society toward women that for several millennia had reduced them to the property of their fathers and husbands: Jesus raised them to partners!

Celibacy and Virginity

The teachings of Paul and his disciples reinforced the emphasis Jesus had placed on chastity and the sanctity of the marriage bond, but Paul forced the theme to an even greater extreme, advocating celibacy for those not yet married. In his view, since the kingdom of God was so imminent, there was no need to marry, although Paul never claimed that he had this teaching from Jesus. Embracing Paul's teaching during the turbulent and dangerous times they lived in, many Christians, both male and female, decided to remain chaste in anticipation of their early death and reunion with Jesus in his "kingdom in heaven."

Faced with persecution and sometimes martyrdom, Christians supported each other with their personal wealth and substance. They took the admonitions of Jesus seriously: "Sell all you have and give it to the poor"(Luke 12.33). They focused on forming a close relationship with the Risen Lord who promised them an eternal reward with him: "Blessed are those persecuted for the sake of righteousness, for theirs is the kingdom of heaven" (Matt. 5.10). Under these circumstances, following the teachings of Paul, who had fully expected the immediate return of Jesus to establish his kingdom on earth, the community emphasized the transcendence of God and the hope of eternal life in a celestial paradise in heaven, disassociating themselves gradually from the joys and blessings of their earthly home. Celibacy of both men and women, nearly unknown and never widely encouraged in Judaism, was the model for holiness that Paul advocated, although it was universally known and acknowledged that the apostles and first generation Jewish converts to Christianity were married, in compliance with Jewish law based on the Torah: "Be fruitful and multiply" (Gen. 1.28).

Virginity gradually became a stated ideal of the Christian community—keeping oneself chaste for the celestial reunion with the eternal Bridegroom of the soul. This thought survives in the final chapter of Revelation, written near the close of the first century, where the "Holy City"—the New Jerusalem of Christians—is arrayed as a Bride for her nuptials with the sacrificed Lamb, the "root and offspring of Judah"—Jesus himself.

Virgin Martyrs

Peter was faced with a serious dilemma. According to the apocryphal Christian text called The Act of Peter, the preeminent apostle was the father of a very beautiful daughter named Petronilla.[3] Warned of possible scandal, the worried father prayed earnestly that his daughter would be paralyzed so that no one would desire to lie with her. In this way Peter preserved his daughter from the taint of sexual encounter and enabled her to die a virgin, a saint, and a martyr. This little anecdote is a "period piece." It clearly reflects the ideal virtues of the community from which it sprang: holy chastity, martyrdom, and union with the eternal Bridegroom in heaven.

The repudiation of sexuality, the mortification of the flesh, and the denial of all earthly desires were the goals of the spiritual life among the persecuted early adherents to Christianity. The Book

of Revelation extols the virtues of the virgins in heaven who spend their days assembled in the celestial throne room praising God.

The Virgin Mary, the exemplar of chastity, pregnant with the Christ Child, visits her elderly and barren cousin Elizabeth, who has the joyful news that she too is having a child. This child, Jesus' cousin, will be known as John the Baptist.

Apocalypse and the Second Coming

Gleaned from the letters of Paul to the various churches, we find that the first generations of Christians believed that the world as they knew it would soon end and that the kingdom of God would then be established by Jesus himself returning in glory to fulfill the promise of the *parousia*, the "Second Coming." This apocalyptic view was promulgated by communities of Christians marginalized and persecuted by the Romans, hunted down and, in many cases, subjected to brutal executions. In response, the faithful strove to become emotionally detached from the pleasures of human relationships and physical well-being, focusing instead on purifying themselves for their death and promised reward: "resurrection in Christ." Tales of martyrs' courageous embrace of violent death inspired new converts to the faith in rising numbers in all corners of the empire.

Adding fuel to fears of the world's imminent demise was a series of cataclysms that befell the Roman Empire in the first century, disasters that Christians attributed to the wrath of God poured out upon Roman tyrants. Earthquakes destroyed Laodicea in 60–61 C.E. and in 64, Rome herself was destroyed by fire—a calamity the emperor Nero blamed on Christians and used as an excuse to torture and execute their entire community.

A medieval German artist portrays the indomitable Saint Margaret. She holds the dragon on a leash with the coils of the thwarted "beast"—now only a subdued symbol of tyranny—around her feet.

Jerusalem fell to Roman legions and the Jewish Temple was destroyed in 70, a disaster that forced many inhabitants of the Holy City to flee. In 79, the massive eruption of the volcano Vesuvius utterly destroyed the coastal resort city of Pompeii, and a grain famine suffered in the year 92 was so severe that the emperor Domitian decreed a reduction in the acreage used for vineyards, providing an increase in the yield of grain to prevent widespread starvation throughout the empire.

Naturally, the teachings and writings of the early Christians reflect the mood of the unsettled times at the turn of the age. Martyrs were idealized. Had not Jesus himself provided the model when he suffered a cruel death by crucifixion inflicted by Roman soldiers, a death usually reserved for criminals and slaves? Christians aspired to follow his holy example, expecting to follow him also into resurrection and eternal life in heaven. Their stories—often bizarre—survived and were told and retold to inspire courage and determination to keep the faith pure and undefiled. Such stories have provided models for faithful commitment to Christ for two millennia—in spite of dungeon, fire, and sword.

The stories of the martyred were often embellished and occasionally reflect an archetypal, almost fairytale quality, like the tale of "little Petronilla" paralyzed to protect her virginity at the express plea of her father. The saints Agnes, Lucy, and Agatha all vowed to remain virgins, refusing to marry pagan suitors or to sacrifice to heathen gods. They suffered martyrdom, but remained faithful to their heavenly Bridegroom. Saint Margaret was the daughter of a pagan priest in Antioch. When Margaret embraced Christianity and pledged herself to perpetual virginity, her father disowned her. While serving as a shepherdess, she attracted the unwanted attentions of a Roman prefect, Olybrius, who sought to make her his concubine. When she rejected him, Olybrius had her brought to trial, where she was sentenced to death if she would not renounce her Christian faith. Standing firm in her commitment, Margaret was cast into flames, but the flames would not consume her. She was then thrown into a cauldron of boiling water, but again emerged unhurt. Finally, it was ordered that she be beheaded. Legend further embellishes her story: a dragon consumed her, but she thwarted him as well—the cross around her neck causing the monster to burst! In art, Saint Margaret is often pictured leading a dragon, or with a subdued dragon crouching at her feet: the symbol of the brutal tyranny that failed in spite of its malicious attempts to defeat her indomitable spirit.

These and numerous other stories were intended to edify and encourage the faithful faced with physical deprivation and even martyrdom by decree of Roman emperors and their officials. In 325 C.E., a period under the rule of the emperor Constantine, Christianity became accepted as the official religion of the empire and, thereafter, the intense oppression of those considered orthodox ceased, although "heretical" Arian and Gnostic Christians and other heterodox groups continued to be hounded and even martyred for centuries—persecuted by orthodox "Roman" Christians!

Gnostic Teachings

Only now, at the beginning of the third Christian millennium, do we have access to the documents and sacred texts of the Gnostic followers of Jesus persecuted by their own Christian brethren. Many of the texts from the Gnostic Nag Hammadi library have a mystical and visionary emphasis, describing the journey of the soul and esoteric or hidden teachings of the Savior. These codices also record a rivalry between Peter and Mary Magdalene, caused by the strong jealousy of Peter toward the woman whom Jesus loved more than the other disciples. This attitude, repeated in several of the Gnostic gospels, seems to reflect the significant rift between the orthodox members of the "Church of Peter" and the Gnostic heretics who honored Mary Magdalene as the companion of the Lord, to whom he confided secret mystical knowledge not shared with his male disciples.

Several of the Gnostic texts ascribe a certain misogyny to Peter, which is probably not historical, but rather, derived from the attitude of the orthodox hierarchy toward women. Historically, it was not Peter, but Paul, whose epistles firmly denied women a teaching role: "Let a woman learn in silence and in all submission. For I do not allow a woman to teach, nor to exercise authority over men. But she is to keep quiet" (1 Tim. 2.11–12). As copies of Paul's epistles were circulated and their teachings adopted and codified, the status given to women in the earliest days of the Church was gradually degraded. The streams of visions and prophecy that are often available to contemplative women devotees of Christ's Way were blocked; an author of one of the Gnostic texts refers to the bishops of the rigid and legalistic orthodox Church as "waterless canals."

This image of the dryness of the orthodox institution is particularly enlightening. In the early fourth century, Christianity had become accepted, and later in that century, the faith was designated the official religion of Rome. The Church adopted the Roman model of government and with it, the insistence on one God, one faith, one baptism, one creed, and one supreme bishop. Differences in interpretation of Scripture and heterodoxy of belief and doctrine were no longer tolerated. There was only one way to God and only the hierarchy of the official Church was now authorized to dispense the sacraments and guide the faithful. Those Christians who embraced alternative beliefs and teachings were gradually silenced. The Spirit of Prophecy and the living "waters of spirit and truth" associated with the free flowing of the Holy Spirit through the community and its members were forced into an "underground stream"— the esoteric traditions of Western civilization. The faith that had begun in chapel-homes became codified in law and concretized in structures— basilicas and churches where the faithful gathered to celebrate the official liturgy of the Church, the Holy Mass.

The image of water in the desert is an important one in Christian symbolism. In the Hebrew Bible, we read in the apocryphal Book of Sirach that instruction and prophecy flow like a stream from Holy Wisdom, "whose thoughts are deeper than the sea, whose counsels are deeper than the great abyss" (Sirach 24.27). The sea and the abyss were both "feminine" in ancient philosophical systems: The name *Mary* in its many forms comes from the word for "ocean," and every child was born from the salt waters of its mother's womb. Among the desert peoples, water was the most precious element of all, a life-giving necessity. Its cooling and refreshing properties were seen as "feminine" properties. In the dualistic system of the Hellenistic world, intuition and second sight were perceived as feminine, "lunar" gifts—as opposed to the "solar" gifts of reason and mental acumen. The symbolic waters of the Spirit flow through the community in the form of prophecy, preaching, teaching, and wise counsel—activities that were often denied to women in orthodox Christian communities following the newly adopted Roman model, which concentrated these activities under the strict control of a hierarchy of male priests.

In contrast to the one-faith, one-creed ideology of the now Roman Church, Jesus imparted a beautiful teaching to the Samaritan woman at the well: "Whoever drinks the water I shall give will never thirst; the water I shall give will become in him a spring of water welling up to eternal life" (John 4.13–14). He does not speak here of bread and wine. The blocking of the waters of the Spirit was a painful consequence of the later rigid patriarchal model adopted by the Church fathers. But there were still many who thirsted for the life-giving water promised by Christ. Many of them sought the desert way, hoping that its austerity and self-denial would lead them to springs of living water.

The Desert Mothers

The mentality that had promoted lifelong virginity, self-denial, and renunciation of worldly wealth and pleasures did not die with the official reversal of religious persecution of Christians. Both men and women continued to seek union with God through contemplative prayer and now pursued voluntary mortification of the flesh and deprivation of food, water, and even sleep. Small communities of the faithful continued to gather to celebrate their faith in the homes of wealthy members of the Church, sometimes even residing together in groups. Daily spiritual practice of the devout in these colonies was characterized by periods of communal and also private contemplative prayer, Scripture study, service to the poor, and often labor at a craft or trade to earn money necessary for the support of the community.

Only gradually these Christians began to feel the cultural encroachment of the pagan empire that now accepted them and, after 325 C.E., embraced their religion. Many felt that the purity of their faith was endangered by pagan influence in the newly mainstreamed institutional Church and felt impelled to perpetuate the struggle against these corrupting pressures. Some

SAYINGS OF THE
DESERT MOTHERS

A teacher ought to be patient, gentle and humble . . . a compassionate lover of souls.
AMMA THEODORA,
(FOURTH CENTURY)

It is not possible to be encompassed by worldly honor and at the same time to bear spiritual fruit.
AMMA SYNCLETICA,
(FIFTH CENTURY)

even felt alienated from the gradual institutionalization of rituals, sacraments, and prayers. Women in large numbers continued to consecrate themselves as virgins, rejecting suitors and confining themselves to limited living quarters in their families' homes. Having presided over their faith communities, often as deaconesses, many devout and consecrated women continued to counsel disciples who sought their spiritual direction. Often their homes became the refuge of their Christian friends, forming early prototypes for later monastic communities.

Of the contemplatives and ascetics who sought to escape from the world, choosing voluntary simplicity, solitude, and austerity, the number of female ascetics drawn to the "desert way" was double that of males.[4] Exhorted by the Scriptures to sell all they had, to pray unceasingly, and to purify the senses and attitudes that were occasions of sin, these ascetics often sought the solitude of cell or cave: They went to the desert, either physically or figuratively, in order to devote their entire lives to prayer. The desert fathers (*abbas*) and mothers (*ammas*) were noted for their wisdom and holiness, often living in severe deprivation and poverty in remote or isolated regions. Their way of living was a harsh existence—buffeted by wind and sand, sleeping on coarsely woven straw or hair mats on a dirt floor and surviving on the most meager vegetarian fare, often consisting only of dried beans and water.

Voluntary denial of the flesh became a way of continuing martyrdom for those who felt the call to the desert way. Drawn away from the noisy distractions of normal city life, their lives were marked by simplicity and austerity—many desert ascetics vowing lifelong silence in addition to poverty and chastity. They cultivated an inner spiritual journey in their makeshift huts outside the city walls or in caves in the wilderness. Occasionally monasteries were built on high rock formations, from which baskets were lowered in order for food to be brought to the community living in isolation.

The names of the desert ammas had been largely forgotten until excavated by recent feminist scholars and theologians. Like those of the martyrs, the stories told of the desert mothers are often stereotypical. An obscure but charming ascetic was Maria the harp player.[5] Drawn to solitude, she abandoned life in Jerusalem and sought refuge and silence in a cave near the Dead Sea, where she lived as a hermit for eighteen years, the ethereal music of her harp wafting gently over the desert. It is claimed that her supply of oil and dried legumes miraculously replenished itself over the years and never ran dry!

Mary Magdalene herself is claimed to have lived isolated in a cave in the mountains east of Marseilles, where, according to medieval legend, angels ministered to her. Another desert saint is Mary of Egypt, whose legend was encountered by Crusaders when they arrived in the East. This dark-skinned saint, "Mary-Gyp," was a former prostitute who had plied her trade on board a ship

Early Christians went to the desert to devote their lives to prayer. These are some of the | humble dwellings that were carved out of tuff pinnacles in Cappadocia, Turkey.

This fresco of Mary Magdalene in the Lower Church of the Basilica | of Saint Francis of Assisi radiates a calm, ethereal beauty.

this false accusation and took responsibility for the child, though she was banished from her monastery and had to live with the child in poverty outside the city walls. Eventually she was reinstated in her community of monks. Imagine their surprise when it was discovered on her deathbed that their "Brother Marinos" was a woman!

Some of the wise women of the desert became herbalists and healers; many more were called upon for intercessory prayer, and the many miraculous cures they effected were the source of their wide renown. Among the desert dwellers, idleness was not tolerated, so many ascetics wove cloth or made baskets to support themselves and distributed their profits to the poor. Their spirituality was practiced quietly, following the scriptural exhortation to pray and give alms in secret. They memorized the Psalms and rejoiced in singing and reciting the Scriptures, which occupied a large part of their day. Many gave spiritual direction to disciples drawn to them by reputation. Their memorable sayings were retained in a strong oral tradition and eventually recorded in various manuscripts describing the lives of these exemplary holy women. Before them was the model of the Mary who had sat at the feet of the Lord listening to his every word, the sister of Lazarus who had "chosen the better part."

that took her to Israel. There she was converted to Christ and repented of her former life, living out her days in solitude as a desert anchorite.

The story of a fifth-century ascetic named Marina has an edifying twist.⁶ With her widowed father, she decided to divest herself of her inheritance and distributed her wealth to the poor. Then, dressed as a man, she entered a monastery with her father. Once, while traveling away from the monastery, she was falsely accused of having fathered a child. In the self-effacing spirit of Christian humility and charity, Marina accepted

PRACTICE: CREATE A SHRINE AND MEDITATION CORNER

Choose a quiet corner in your house, preferably with room for a comfortable chair (or mat for sitting on the floor) and a small table, desk, or corner cabinet. You may want to cover the surface of the table with a cloth or mat of some sort—woven, crocheted, or embroidered.

Select a picture or statue of Jesus or, if you prefer, the Virgin Mary or another favorite saint. Remembering that each saint represents specific virtues and strengths, you may decide to have more than one icon on your altar or cabinet—perhaps a group of paintings of several different sizes and a statue or two. Choose icons that are meaningful for you.

Another nice touch for your meditation corner is a small bouquet of seasonal or dried flowers, or a flowering plant. These can be changed at will, perhaps substituting a bowl of fruit or a potpourri of dried rose petals. A candle should be placed on the altar, a reminder of Christ, the "Light of the world." When you visit your shrine for prayer or meditation, you may want to put on some devotional music, chanting, or orchestral pieces. Before assuming a comfortable position near your altar to begin your meditation, light your candle, making sure that it is safely ensconced in a fireproof container.

A statue or painting that has a significance for you, such as this intimate and prayerful study of the Blessed Virgin Mary, will help to focus your meditation.

CHAPTER THREE

SERENITY, SERVICE, AND SIMPLICITY

*Peace I leave with you, my peace I give to you . . . let not
your heart be troubled or be afraid.*

(JOHN 14.27)

Serenity, Service, and Simplicity

Several feminine aspects of the Sacred are celebrated in Christianity, the heritage of those who adopted the maxims and parables of Jesus, accepted them literally, and made them "flesh" by living them on a daily basis—walking the spiritual path of service to others, singing songs of praise and thanksgiving, and seeking communion with God in silent prayer. Although their practice was personal and intimate, it often provided visionary and prophetic insight that nurtured the faith of the wider community of believers. As the practice of the official Roman Church became more circumscribed and institutionalized, the monastic system that grew out of the communal experience of the desert ascetics served to form a counterbalance, cultivating the immediate experience of God's intimate love and communion with each individual soul.

The monastic tradition provided a quiet sanctuary for both women and men who wished to devote their lives to God. The passive or "feminine" virtues of silence, compassion, and voluntary simplicity were fostered in these communities isolated from the hectic bustle of the cities of the Roman Empire. During the first three centuries of Christianity, the faith was centered in regions washed by the Mediterranean Sea where missionaries had spread the *kerygma*, or "proclamation" of salvation in Christ, baptizing new converts in the name of the Father, the Son, and the Holy Spirit—the Holy Trinity. During the fourth century, the publicly encouraged religion spread rapidly

from the great imperial cities of Rome and Constantinople to the far outposts of the Roman Empire, through Gaul to the northern forests of the Germanic tribes and to the British Isles, gradually supplanting the cult of Mithras popular among the Roman legions occupying these remote regions. From the sandswept deserts of northern Africa, the faith found its way by sea to the coast of Spain and from there to the isolated shores of Ireland, where it encountered and became amalgamated with the indigenous culture of the Celts, among whom the Sacred Feminine was traditionally honored as the "Three Ladies." The native Celts of Ireland valued the feminine attributes of wisdom, intuition, and experience of the senses. In this remote haven, far from the marble pillars of imperial Rome, a unique marriage of Christian doctrine and native culture produced a faith that retained the original egalitarian flavor of the very earliest Christian communities—a faith rooted in the parables of Jesus and the literal application of his maxims in the ascetic practice of serenity, simplicity, and service, virtues practiced in the abbeys founded by Christians in the hearts of their villages.

Celtic Christianity

The Druidic civilization of the indigenous Celtic tribes was rural, tribal, and agrarian. It valued "feminine" streams of mysticism, poetry, and prophecy, while honoring the immanence of the Divine indwelling all creation. Irish abbeys inherited the traditions of the bardic schools of

The Celtic cross is seen in the the cemetery of Templebrady, Cork, in southern Ireland. Irish abbeys inherited the traditions of their Druid forebears, along with the Celtic aware-ness of the beauty and diversity of nature itself.

their Druid forebears along with the Celtic awareness of the world of nature in all its beauty and diversity. Hospitality and community were very important in this nonhierarchal society that celebrated the kinship of all creation and the inherent goodness of the earth and nature. They sensed the integral connectedness of the earth and all her children: The gardener cares for the garden and the garden cares for the gardener. Pantheism underlay their faith: They sensed that God was active in every aspect of creation, an attitude that later was to influence the continental mystics Hildegard of Bingen and Meister Eckhardt.

May the road rise with you.
May the wind be always at your back.
May the sun shine warm upon your face.
May the rain fall soft upon your fields,
And until we meet again,
May God hold you
in the hollow of his hand.
(IRISH BLESSING)

honor of the purification of the Virgin Mary forty days after the birth of her child. Samhain, the day when the Celts celebrated their connection with the spirits of their ancestors and the Underworld, was renamed "All Saints Day." Bride, the ancient patron goddess of Ireland, who was often identified with the land herself, was subsumed into "Saint Brigid," her fifth-century namesake who became an important abbess, founder of the convent of Cill-Dara, "the church of the oak." The town that grew up around her center of learning later became the cathedral town of Kildare, and the abbess Brigid became a legend of charisma and sanctity. She was honored as a friend in "great charity" of Saint Patrick himself. Her feast day, February 1, coincides not accidentally with the ancient Imbolc festival dedicated to Bride, the Celtic goddess. Numerous wells, springs, and other landmarks in Ireland still bear her name.

While Saint Patrick is often credited with converting the Irish to Christianity, history testifies that much of Ireland was Christian long before his arrival. The fifth century monk-theologian Pelagius, believed by many scholars to have been Irish, insisted on the goodness of creation and the free will of people to make their own choices. Pelagius believed that sin could not be hereditary; it was a choice a person was able to make because of God's gracious gift of free will. He came into conflict with Augustine, who was promulgating the doctrine of Original Sin deriving from the sin of Adam and Eve. Augustine was able to convince the pope that Pelagius "the Scot" (a term often used to mean an Irishman) was a heretic, and in 418

In ancient times these fertile fields in Ireland may have been dedicated to Bride, the patron goddess of the land, who was later subsumed into Saint Brigid of Kildare, the female patron of the Church in Ireland.

For the Irish, all life was sacred, all ground was holy ground.

Missionaries to Ireland built their stone churches on the isle's ancient holy sites, Christianized Druidic practices, and renamed Druid festivals in honor of Christian holy days. The Celtic feast of Imbolc—the feast of the quickening of the earth, celebrated since ancient times as a day for burning off the chaff of the former year's crops to purify the fields for replanting—became "Candlemas" in

Pelagius was excommunicated, thirteen years before Saint Patrick arrived to evangelize the natives of the emerald isle.

While Celtic traditions were inclusive, egalitarian, and based on the practice of servant leadership, Rome's Christian missionaries tried to impose structure, uniformity, and authority—their "one pope, one faith, one creed" model—on the institutions of their Irish converts. Faced with Rome's emphasis on the power of God the Father and the authority of Jesus the Son, Irish converts were more inclined to be Trinitarian, honoring the Holy Spirit with a special intensity. The indigenous flavor of Celtic Christianity actually prevailed to a surprising degree, probably because of the sheer distance of Irish hamlets and abbeys from Rome. However, at the Synod of Whitby in 664 the Celtic/Irish church submitted to the pope's emissaries, finally accepting Rome's date for Easter, which had been a source of contention. Over the next several centuries, the distinctively Irish faith and practice was gradually subsumed into the Roman model, subject to Roman authorities for whom obedience was the preeminent virtue.

Gradually, during a period of several centuries, Ireland became a prominent repository of Christian wisdom. Tucked away in quiet corners of their monasteries, Irish copyists labored with quill and ink to preserve sacred texts for posterity during a period when Vikings from the north were raiding towns and religious compounds, and terrorizing the populations of coastal areas of Britain and the continent. The remote isolation of Ireland made her abbeys a refuge where

I arise today
Through the strength of heaven
Light of sun
Radiance of moon
Splendor of fire
Speed of lightning
Swiftness of wind
Depth of sea
Stability of earth
Firmness of rock . . .
I arise today
Through God's strength to pilot me:
God's might to uphold me,
God's wisdom to guide me,
God's eyes to look before me,
God's ear to hear me,
God's word to speak for me,
God's hand to guard me,
God's way to lie before me,
God's shield to protect me,
God's host to save me
From snares of devils,
From temptations of vices,
From every one who shall wish me ill,
Afar and anear,
Alone and in a multitude.

(SAINT PATRICK FROM "THE DEER'S CRY," TR. KUNO MEYER[7])

scholarship and civilization managed to survive and even thrive during the Dark Ages. Illuminated manuscripts were the product of scriptoria in dual

The Virgin and Child depicted in the Book of Kells, one of the most important of the Irish illuminated manuscripts.

monasteries, where women as well as men were educated in the great centers of learning that flourished on Irish soil. Beautiful drawings of flora and fauna in bright colored inks decorate manuscripts copied in Irish abbeys, while others are covered with lovely intricate designs that illustrate the interconnectedness of all creation. The Book of Kells survives among other examples of this highly developed art. While the Judeo-Christian Scriptures were copied in Latin, the old pagan sagas were preserved in Gaelic. Irish religious communities also preserved the oral tradition of the ancient bards who had memorized their poems. They sang or chanted prayers and litanies, often singing while working in the fields or walking the narrow paths between villages. Several distinctive features characterize Celtic prayer: It was intimate, informal, spontaneous, and poetic, often with imagery from home or nature. It was often a grateful expression of the immanence of God and the sense of being in the Holy presence—through the Holy Spirit's indwelling of one's own heart.

Monastic Tradition

Religious life in the monastic system offered women a refuge from the traditional roles of wife and mother, often lived out in poverty and drudgery and culminating in an early death in childbirth. Christian parents often dedicated daughters to God at a young age, and many older women were drawn to religious communities after their childrearing years were over, or when they were left widows. Often Irish couples made a mutual decision to separate and to take religious vows after their children were grown and married, while others elected to go on pilgrimage to holy shrines, many traveling as far as Rome or Jerusalem. When the great Irish missionaries embarked on their journeys to spread Christianity to the barbarian tribes on the continent, they took with them the vibrant Christianity of their island, with its unique union of the ancient Celtic values—the interconnectedness of all creation and the immanence of God's presence—with the doctrines, order, and authority of Roman Catholicism. It was this faith that spread through the monasteries of continental Europe, sparking a spiritual revival and bringing streams of light to dispel the Dark Ages.

Christian learning and civilization cultivated in Ireland's monasteries spread first to Scotland and England; here, they gradually converted the Germanic Angle and Saxon conquerors of Britain and were carried eastward by English and Irish missionary monks—to Germany by Boniface, to Burgundy, Swabia, and Lombardy by Columban, to France by Alcuin—eventually consolidating the religious life of Europe under the hegemony of the Roman Catholic pope.

On the European continent it was the Benedictine monasteries that filled the vacuum left by the disintegration of the Roman schools and institutions in western Europe. Founded by the Italian saint, Benedict of Nursia (c.480–543), the order had flourished. Its discipline was based on the fundamental tenet that work was prayer, and the monks and nuns who made up the Benedictine orders followed Benedict's Rule centered on the Divine Office. The day was divided into eight equal parts so that every three hours the religious community was called to a period of prayer when Psalms of the Hebrew Bible

Christ with me,

Christ before me,

Christ behind me,

Christ in me,

Christ beneath me,

Christ above me,

Christ on my right,

Christ on my left,

Christ when I lie down,

Christ when I sit down,

Christ when I arise,

Christ in the heart of every

man who thinks of me,

Christ in the mouth of every

one who speaks of me,

Christ in every eye that

sees me,

Christ in every ear that

hears me.

("SAINT PATRICK'S BREAST-PLATE," TR. KUNO MEYER[8])

were sung or chanted, so a continuous rhythm of prayer, work, and study was maintained within the monastery walls. Benedict is credited with founding a dozen monasteries in Europe, and from these foundations the order based on his Rule spread across the continent, creating secure oases of learning and culture in the midst of the turmoil of the barbarian onslaughts.

While Rome crumbled, civilization did manage to survive. Eventually the fresh breeze of Celtic Christianity met with the Rule of Saint Benedict and they joined hands. The only stable Western institution was the Church; its Latin was the language of the learned, confined to clergy and those educated in monastic schools. It is in these schools and monasteries, notably Aachen where Alcuin taught in the school established by Charlemagne, St. Gall in Swabia, and Monte Cassino, that the flicker of the light of civilization was nursed through the darkest hours and fanned into an ever stronger and brighter flame. These monasteries were self-contained and self-sufficient. Benedictine nuns and monks took vows of chastity, poverty, and obedience; they tilled the land, baked the bread, brewed ale, cultivated crops, copied the sacred texts of their faith and came together to chant the Divine Office, nurturing the flame of Divine Love at the heart of the Christian faith. Their stout walls gave protection from the recurring invasions of Vandals, Vikings, and Huns.

Be Thou my Vision
O Lord of my heart,
Naught be all else to me
Save that Thou art—
Thou my best thought
By day or by night,
Waking or sleeping,
Thy presence, my light.[9]

Hilda of Whitby

Occasionally the spiritual flame flared up with great intensity in the lives and teachings of charismatic Christian religious, many of whom were women. Hilda of Whitby was a teen convert to the Celtic Christianity that had spread to England. Single until the age of thirty, she then took monastic vows and founded several double monasteries housing monks and nuns on the Irish model, probably influenced by the fifth-century dual abbey of Saint Victor founded by John Cassian in Marseilles, where both male and female religious were housed. Hilda was renowned for her intellect, charity, and justice. Her monastery at Whitby became an important center of learning where she herself taught music, grammar, theology, and even medicine. Scholars suggest she was ordained a bishop in the Celtic tradition before she hosted the Synod of Whitby in 664, at which the Irish church submitted itself to Roman authority and control. This outcome of the synod must have saddened her deeply, since Rome's Christianity was more legalistic, rigid, judgmental, and patriarchal than that of the Irish missionaries who had established communities of converts in England.

Hrotswitha of Gandersheim

A later medieval nun, Hrotswitha of Gandersheim (c. 935–999), founded her own monastery at Gandersheim, just south of Hanover, Germany, and was probably a canoness rather than an abbess, a position that would have allowed her to own property, entertain guests, and move freely about the country. She was highly educated for a woman of her time. In her writings, she mentions that one of her most influential teachers was Gerberga, a niece of the holy Roman emperor Otto I. Hrotswitha was an author of some talent whose plays centered on the lives of women. In *Gallicanus*, the pagan officer who demands the hand of a Christian virgin Constantia in marriage is converted and dies a Christian martyr. In *Calimachus*, a Christian wife and her lover die and are restored to life by the prayers of John the Apostle. *Sapientia*, an allegory, describes a mother's grief at the loss of her virgin daughters, Faith, Hope, and Charity. Hrotswitha's highly regarded play entitled *Abraham* celebrates the conversion of a harlot by a monk disguised as a lover. When confronted by a bishop who did not like the flavor and humor of her plays, Hrotswitha's cheerful reply was, "At least they have pleased myself!"

Hildegard of Bingen

Connectedness with the beauty and abundant gifts of the earth was deeply embedded in the writings of the German visionary Hildegard of Bingen (1098–1179), botanist, philosopher, theologian, and healer. Sequestered at eight years of age, a child anchorite in a tiny cell, Hildegard later outgrew her narrow confines and became one of the most well known of all medieval women mystics. Her mentor, the anchoress Jutta, taught the frail and sickly daughter of minor nobility to read and sing psalms in Latin, encouraging her to develop a talent for music that later blossomed into her own musical compositions. Medieval anchorites were obliged to remain in their cells until death, but an exception was made in the case of Hildegard. She began having ecstatic visions at an early age, and, as news of her spirituality, intellect, and talent spread throughout the Rhine district, more women were drawn to share her cell, which eventually became a convent. Hildegard herself was permitted to leave her cell to become a nun in the community. Eventually, she took over leadership of the community and became prioress of the Benedictine cloister of Diessenberg in 1136, founding a second convent across the Rhine in Rupertsburg around 1147–50. So widespread was Hildegard's fame that during her own lifetime this amazing woman was known as "the Sibyl of the Rhine."

I saw a very bright fire which was incomprehensible, inextinguishable, wholly living, and appearing as if it was totally alive.
(HILDEGARD OF BINGEN[10])

Relying on her scribe, the monk Volmer, Hildegard's literary works include mystery plays, poems, and a book of saints' lives. She recorded her prophetic and apocalyptic visions in a book called *Scivias* (1141–52) and two further books of visions. When her spiritual director requested that she not continue recording her visions, Hildegard replied that she could not stop because God requested that she continue to record them. She found it necessary to obey God rather than her spiritual director.

Perhaps her own history of ill health prompted Hildegard's passionate interest in medical science. Her vast knowledge of herbs and their healing properties as well as other aspects of her wisdom were gathered experientially and through her visions. She was intensely interested in holistic healing and is the author of an extensive medical treatise, *Hildegardis Curae et Causae*, five books on treating the human body and the causes, symptoms, and treatment of human disease. Another treatise, *Liber Simplicis Medicinae*, consists of nine books. These books cover plants, trees, stones, fishes, birds, quadrupeds, reptiles, metals, and elements—a set that makes up a complete natural history!

Considering the medieval emphasis on the spiritual realm and its relative neglect of the flesh and the earthly realm, it appears surprising that Hildegard could have written such colossal works dealing with nature and the physical world. Undoubtedly, these works are an outgrowth of her firm belief that God loved and delighted in the beauty and diversity manifested throughout the entire cosmos—the "mirror" of divinity. Hildegard explains the word *viriditas*, the "greenness" or life principle of the universe. She is a great favorite with modern environmental groups—as a pioneer scientist fascinated by the variety and intricacy found in nature and the interconnectedness of all creation. Her works are a hymn to the "moist" and ever "greening" life force of the Creator.

*Would'st thou grasp
my meaning?
Lie down in the Fire.
See and savor the
Divinity
Flowing through
thy being.*

(MECHTILD OF MAGDEBURG,
THE FLOWING LIGHT
OF THE GODHEAD, 6.29)

Mechtild of Magdeburg

Hildegard of Bingen's overwhelming visionary experience of being immersed in brilliant light is often described by mystics and is very similar to an experience recounted a century later by her countrywoman, Mechtild of Magdeburg, in *The Flowing Light of the Godhead*, a work that takes us inside the unitive experience of the contemplative.

Adopting the powerful and appealing metaphor of Christ as Bridegroom so highly developed by Saint Bernard (c. 1090–1153) in his commentary on the Song of Songs, the religious orders of monastics were fundamentally transformed. The rigid order and rules of militarisitic religious orders were inevitably softened as both nuns and monks turned to the Beloved for solace and inspiration. Before the eternal Bridegroom, each individual soul was cast in the role of Bride. No one has expressed this relationship more passionately than Mechtild of Magdeburg (c. 1210–1297) who carried on an intense, personal, and intimate romance with God. Because we know almost nothing about her life, we rely on her book to tell us of her mystical experience. Her writing style is a stream of consciousness, her vernacular German dialect full of erotic language and sensual imagery. It is the language of courtly love, and Jesus, her Redeemer, is her ardent lover. She speaks of the Holy Spirit as a wellspring, a source of flowing light and love imbuing the soul. It is the *minneflut*—a "flowing stream" of love infusing her with passion for God, filling her with desire for mystical union with the Beloved.

Mechtild employs feminine terms of nurture and compassion. Wine, tears, water, milk, and honey flow from us in our charity and concern for others, and God refills our vessel with his own flowing light of love. Her mystical experience of her Beloved is lyrical and sensual, and her book is a classic expression of contemplative union coming directly from the heart. She speaks of her body as a beloved prison in which she is bound, but she does not reject her flesh in the tradition of ascetic mystics. She honored the human incarnation of the Divine in Jesus and was a devotee also of the Virgin Mary who had "suckled" the apostles with her fervent prayers and maternal teachings. For Mechtild, God was both immanent, infusing his Bride—the soul—with love, and transcendent, above every throne. One of her most appealing images of her relationship with God was her perceived role as his *hausfrau*, or "housewife"—a domestic and loving wife characterized by willing service and tender devotion to her spouse.

Catherine of Siena

The spirituality of these visionary women spread out from their convents into the wider world, influencing the faith of their contemporaries and later generations of religious mystics. One of the most extraordinary of them all was Catherine Benincasa of Siena, the twenty-fourth child of her parents, a surviving twin. Even as a child, she practiced severe self-denial and pursued passionate interior prayer. In reaction to Catherine's interest in the spiritual life, her well-to-do parents forced her to do housework, treating her like a servant.

Catherine's response was to serve her family and siblings in a spirit of cheerful cooperation and to go ever deeper into the sanctuary of her own interior prayer-cell. Scarred in her youthful years by a severe case of chickenpox, Catherine was accepted into the third order of Dominicans at sixteen and immersed herself in spiritual practices of self-denial and solitude, rarely venturing outside her room except to attend Mass at the Dominican cloister near her home. When she was twenty, after more than three years of seclusion, she received a vision in which Jesus told her that she must henceforth serve her neighbor, finding him present in others. Catherine emerged from her cell and began to take part in her family's busy life, again taking the role of a servant, doing their laundry and nursing them in illness and infirmity, even during periods of plague that swept through Siena, ravaging its population.

Catherine was sought out for her wisdom in spiritual counseling and mediation of difficult relationships, and became widely renowned in her own lifetime, constantly in demand for intercessory prayer and arbitration of onerous cases. In one instance, she pressed Pope Gregory XI to leave the court of the "Babylonian Captivity" in Avignon and return to Rome, where he died soon afterward, leaving the politics of the papacy in abysmal partisan turmoil in spite of Catherine's best efforts at reconciling the factions. Miraculous healings are attributed to her intercession, including that of her personal spiritual director and dearest friend, Blessed Raymond Capua. Her monumental spiritual work, *Dialogue,* contains her entire experience of the spiritual life, dictated in the vernacular Italian and recorded by three scribes working in shifts. Raymond remarked of her: "Catherine carried the whole Church in her heart." Her fasting was so intense that she literally could not eat or sleep for several years before her death and was a walking wraith, whose internal spirit burned so intensely and passionately with love for Christ and his people that she did not notice physical pain. She died in 1380, at the age of thirty-three and, in 1970, was declared a Doctor of the Roman Catholic Church, one of its most remarkable sanctified women.

Teresa of Avila

Two later Christian mystics, both named Teresa, removed by centuries from these early medieval mothers of the mystical way, deserve our attention. The first of these was the Carmelite Teresa of Avila (1515–1582), cherished friend of Saint John of the Cross, with whom she worked to reform a Carmelite order grown lax in its practice of spiritual discipline. Of all the famous visionaries, Teresa seems to have been one of the most worldly. She was unusually beautiful and very lively as a teenager and, soon, after indulging in a romantic liaison with a cousin, was

Teresa of Avila discusses three fundamental aspects of prayer: The first is mutual charity; the second is complete detachment from all creation; while the third is authentic humility, which . . . embraces all others.

(WAY OF PERFECTION, 4.4)

Saint Catherine of Siena received a vision in which Jesus told her that she must serve her neighbor, finding him present in others. Catherine was sought out for her words of wisdom in spiritual counseling and was a skilled mediator as well as a healer and mystic.

placed by her worried father in a strict convent school. There, to her own surprise, she was happy and found herself considering a religious vocation. She returned to her home, helped her widowed father care for her younger siblings, and then, against his objections, presented herself at the age of twenty as a novice to the Carmelite Sisters of the Incarnation in Avila.

As a member of the religious order, Teresa did not mortify her flesh or seek strict seclusion. By reason of her generous dowry, she was assigned a small suite of rooms as her living quarters, although the poorer sisters lived in tight conditions in a dormitory. At twenty-three, she became so ill that she was given leave of absence to return to her family to regain her health. But a further illness resulted in a coma that lasted for four days and left her paralyzed for several years. She had to learn to crawl again and then to walk. She returned to her convent and eventually recovered her health, although never fully. Teresa later described her spiritual journey in her *Autobiography* and amplified her description of her internal method of mental prayer in her second book, *Way of Perfection*, an intimate discourse addressed to her sisters in the convent of Saint Joseph. Teresa was an observant judge of human character and foible and was able to develop a rule for her order that respected and honored the sisters, refusing to inflict cruel punishments and privations upon them.

Under the scrutiny of the diligent and repressive Spanish Inquisition, she managed to instruct her fellow nuns in the contemplative life during an era when women were forbidden to preach or teach. The Inquisition was ever alert to heresy, especially among converted Jews and women, and Teresa's half-Jewish heritage made her doubly suspect when reports of her unusual intellect, charisma, and contemplative prayer became known outside her community.

Teresa's first encounter with the principles of mental prayer came from an encounter during her early illness with a classic treatise on the subject entitled *The Third Spiritual Alphabet* by Francisco de Osuna. After recovering from her nearly fatal illness, she went through a period of spiritual dryness that lasted until she was forty, when she was suddenly overcome by an emotional conversion experience that immediately restored and increased her personal intimacy with her Bridegroom, whom she called "His Majesty" in her writings. Disturbed by the lax practices in the Convent of the Incarnation, Teresa established a reformed community under a stricter rule at the Convent of Saint Joseph and, in all, seventeen other reformed cloisters and four monasteries. Her deep friendship with Saint John of the Cross and their combined efforts to reform the Carmelite order bore fruit, in spite of the politics

Myrrh-bearers still—
at home, abroad,
What paths have
holy women trod,
Burdened with
votive gifts for God.
(MARGARET JUNKIN
PRESTON, *MYRRH-*
BEARERS[11])

Ask and you shall receive; seek and you shall
find; knock, and it shall be opened to you.
If you . . . know how to give good gifts, how
much more will your heavenly Father give the
Holy Spirit to those who ask him?

(LUKE 11.9, 13)

of the time that imposed obstacles in their path, including the kidnap and imprisonment of John. Although ill health accompanied Teresa throughout her life, she did not allow it to prevent her from accomplishing her work for Jesus: the advancement of contemplative prayer and union with the eternal Bridegroom, the source of her joy and strength. In her final work, *The Interior Castle*, she describes the soul as a beautiful diamond or crystal with many rooms—seven dwelling places that symbolize the seven stages of contemplative prayer. Like other mystics, Teresa often employs the language of courtship, betrothal, and marriage in her spiritual discourse. Always wary of possible censure by Inquisitors who protected the traditional faith centered on the Mass and the Eucharist, Teresa carefully instructs and guides her readers into the unitive experience of God within—the constant and intimate conversation with the Beloved dwelling in one's innermost being.

Patience achieves the goal.
Whoever has God wants for nothing.
God alone fills her every need.

(TERESA OF AVILA)

Thérèse of Lisieux

Although both have received the title "Doctor of the Roman Catholic Church," the contrast of Thérèse of Lisieux with the Spanish reformer of their Carmelite order whose name she bore is superficially stark. The Spanish mystic lived a long and productive life; her nineteenth-century French follower died at a youthful twenty-four. While Teresa was charming, vivacious, and outgoing, a bit wild and worldly during her youth, Thérèse Martin was painfully shy and scrupulously obedient as a child, commiting herself to Christ at the age of nine. She was the last child of her devout and aging parents. Her mother, a lacemaker, was forty-two when Thérèse was born and died of breast cancer when the baby was four. The bereaved husband moved his family to Lisieux and continued to raise his children in an environment of intense piety, encouraging all five of his surviving daughters to enter the religious life. The two older sisters, Pauline and Marie, both in their teens, raised and mentored the two youngest siblings after the death of their mother. Little Thérèse suffered from depression and intense shyness, which

One of the most popular Roman Catholic saints, Thérèse of Lisieux was admitted to the Carmelite order at the age of fifteen and devoted her short life to Jesus. Although she considered herself to be "a simple child," she was declared a Doctor of the Church a century after her death.

*Our Lord needs
neither our great
actions nor our
profound ideas; neither
our mental ability
nor our talents. He
loves simplicity.*

(SAINT THÉRÈSE OF LISIEUX,
THE STORY OF A SOUL)

increased when she started school, where she felt intimidated and very miserable. When she was nine, her beloved sister Pauline entered the Carmelite convent. Faced with this irrevocable loss, Thérèse responded by becoming ill with uncontrollable chills, fever, and convulsions that lasted for some months.

Eventually she was cured of the physical symptoms by a smile from the Blessed Virgin Mary, but Thérèse remained timorous and overconcerned about achieving perfection, becoming excruciatingly scrupulous in her zeal, a temperament that worried her sisters.

At Christmas when she was thirteen, she experienced an encounter with pure charity that established balance in her life, allowing her to delight in her schoolwork and providing her with a vocation to save souls. Already at nine, when Pauline had been accepted into the convent, Thérèse had experienced a call to the religious life, and at fifteen she was finally permitted to join the Carmelite cloister in Lisieux. Here she was reunited with two of her sisters and devoted the remaining years of her short life to pleasing Jesus in little ways. She compared her little acts of service and obedience to flowers offered to her Beloved Christ, and is identified with her "little way" of simple abandonment to God and the careful accomplishment of small duties for love of Jesus.

She died of tuberculosis in 1897, was later canonized, and in 1997 was declared a Doctor of the Roman Catholic Church by Pope John Paul II. No one would have been more thoroughly surprised by this honorific title than Thérèse herself! She considered herself a simple child, offering her small duties and services for the salvation of souls and to give pleasure and comfort to Jesus. Thérèse is widely known as the "Little Flower of Jesus" and draws countless Christians to practice her "little way."

Thérèse composed numerous poems and canticles to Jesus but only reluctantly wrote her autobiography in response to the demand of her convent's mother superior. The book, *The Story of a Soul*, describes the spiritual journey of her "little way" and has become a classic. It is the careful attention to small and simple tasks done as conscious acts of love that manifests a uniquely "feminine" spirituality that is heartfelt and spontaneous.

Christian mystics and scholars helped to keep the passionate fire of love and compassion burning brightly in their communities throughout Europe, the heirs of both the order and the discipline of the monastic tradition and the Scripture-based prayer of the contemplative ascetics. The diversity of their experience testifies to the breadth in God and is underscored by their similarity. All were utterly and wholly devoted to God and poured their love out at his feet, very like Mary—the passionate woman with the alabaster jar of nard, who poured her precious unguent out on the feet of Jesus and dried them with her hair.

PRACTICE:
A SPIRITUAL JOURNAL

Life is an incredible journey, and so special that it deserves to be lived carefully and with reflection. In an earlier practice, we mentioned recording insights in a journal, but now we suggest that if you haven't already created a journal, you might want to take time to do so. You can buy a journal with a beautiful cover and blank sheets, or you can take an ordinary looseleaf notebook and create a fabric or special paper cover for it. Let the colors, style, and decorations reflect your personal mood.

There are no strict rules about journaling, but there are several fundamental guidelines: Whatever you write, let it be the truth. Perhaps you may want to choose a Psalm or other passage from Scripture as a starting point for focusing your thoughts. Record your dreams if you wish, or something perceived in a meditation period. Many may find it beneficial to write questions that they find perplexing or bothering. Then, perhaps at some later date, when your question has been answered, you can record the answer and how it was perceived.

Journaling is a wonderful way to get in touch with your innermost emotions, hopes, and desires. Be sure to keep your journal in a safe place of utmost privacy so you will feel free to write honestly about even intimate problems without fear of having these thoughts seen by others. This journal will contain the story of your soul and its journey under the guidance of the "traveling companion"—the Holy Spirit.

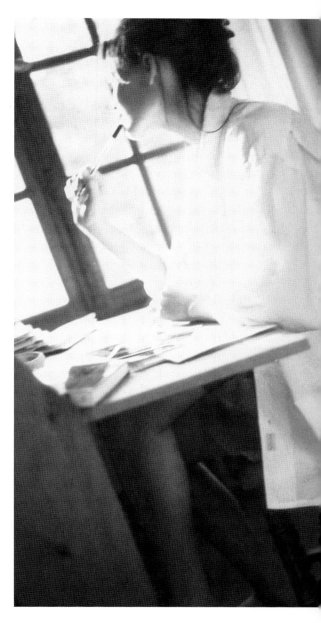

Creating a spiritual journal that focuses on your prayers, thoughts, and dreams can set you on the road toward achieving a connection with your inner self. The Holy Spirit will be your guide on this intimate and revealing journey.

CHAPTER FOUR

THE SACRED JOURNEY

I am the way, the truth, and the life.

(JOHN 14.6)

The Sacred Journey

Pilgrimage is a metaphor for the sacred journey of the soul toward union with God—the age-old quest for the Beloved/Other that seems to be centered in the longing of the human heart for fulfillment and completion. The journey to a holy site is the outward manifestation of the inner path of purification and transformation. It is rooted in a narrative found in the Book of Exodus—the story of the chosen people traveling out of Egypt across the Red Sea and into the desert, finally attaining the Promised Land. In Christianity, the traditional food for the spiritual journey is the manna of the Holy Eucharist, consecrated during the ritual of the Mass. This is the "Bread of Life"—Christ himself. For many Christians, the manna is the words of the Holy Scripture which nourishes them: "Thy words were found and I did eat them" (Jer. 15.16). And again: "I have esteemed the words of his mouth more than my necessary food" (Job 23.12).

Until the Protestant Reformation of the sixteenth century, western Europe was united under the hegemony of the Roman Catholic Church; her institutions were a ubiquitous presence, and her teachings universally accepted and propagated. While the Divine Liturgy of the Holy Mass was at the heart of Christian worship, the seven sacraments of the Church were dispensed by priests to the faithful as outward signs of Christ's grace in their lives. These rites highlighted special events in the life of a Christian—Baptism, Confirmation, the Eucharist, Reconciliation, Holy Orders, Matrimony, and Extreme Unction, the anointing of the severely ill or dying. Since only ordained priests were allowed to administer these liturgical rites, devout Christians remained close to their Church in order to receive the special blessings and rites of passage that helped to unify all members into one body, the mystical Body of Christ. According to its doctrine, this "Body" included those on earth (the "Church militant"), the saints in heaven (the "Church triumphant"), and the suffering souls in purgatory (those who had not yet attained heavenly union with God). Outside the Church, there was no salvation. In the mid-twelfth century, The Lateran Council officially proclaimed the doctrine of transubstantiation: the action of a Roman Catholic priest was needed to change the ordinary bread and wine of the Eucharist into the physical body and blood of Jesus. This doctrine, along with a Church law that required attendance at Mass on Sundays and confession of sins to a priest at least once a year, further consolidated the power of the Roman Catholic clergy over the people. Concurrently, the pope proclaimed the demand for priestly celibacy, further disassociating priests from the people they served, but securing Church lands and property in the control of the hierarchy. The power and influence of the institutional Church and its doctrines permeated every aspect of medieval society in western Europe.

Great attention and honor were given to Mary, the mother of Jesus, and to the many saints and martyrs whose examples of piety and devotion to Christ were highly honored by the faithful. Devotions offered to these saints included novenas—

Processions to celebrate important events in the life of Jesus have been part of the life of the Church since the Middle Ages. These young people carrying a crucifix are part of a Good Friday procession in Costa Rica.

liturgies repeated for nine consecutive days—and sacramental actions: the blessing of homes, animals, harvests, and fishing vessels in the name of the patron saint. Processions and festivals were declared to celebrate important events in the life of Jesus and his mother, and feast days were established in honor of the most popular saints. The "folk" have always perceived visits made to graves and relics of deceased holy men and women as meritorious. Frequently the supplications of pilgrims made to contemporary holy persons were answered in miraculous fashion, providing a foundation for the eventual canonization of an exceptional candidate for this honor, most often a member of a religious order, and usually a celibate male priest or monk. Sacramentals—crucifixes and holy icons—were highly venerated, along with relics of various saints housed in Christian churches throughout Europe and the Middle East—a bone, a garment, or an instrument of the saint's torture. The shroud of Jesus and fragments of the true cross, the nails that pierced his hands and feet, the chalice of the Last Supper, the tunic or shift of the Blessed Virgin, the finger of one saint, the femur of another—anything related to a saint in any way was honored as sacred by medieval believers. Saints' graves and relics housed at various sanctuaries became the popular objects of veneration and pilgrimage.

While visits to honor famous philosophers and sacred sites were known in the classical world and among the Celtic Druids, the practice of pilgrimage seems to have reached a crescendo in the Middle Ages, when people of all ages flocked in a steady stream to important sacred sites. For Christians, the preeminent pilgrimage destination was Jerusalem. Although the Muslim Arabs had conquered the Holy City in 637, they honored Jesus as a prophet and, in a perhaps surprising spirit of ecumenism, had continued to allow Christians to visit the Holy City and its sacred sites: Bethlehem, Golgotha, the Garden of Gethsemane, and the Holy Sepulcher. Religious orders had built and continuously maintained hospices along the way from Europe to Jerusalem in order to accommodate increasing numbers of pilgrims to the Holy Land who wished to visit the city where their Lord had suffered crucifixion and been raised from the dead. Contemporary accounts record journeys of women and children as well as men to the eastern shores of the Mediterranean. For many, pilgrimage was a family affair.

The Crusades and the Cultural Renaissance

In the late eleventh century, when Europe was gradually emerging from the barbarisms of the Dark Ages and beginning to establish stronger civic communities under the aegis of their feudal lords, conditions in the Middle East were rapidly deteriorating. Warring Turkish and Muslim armies made travel in the region precarious, and pilgrimage was interrupted. With an eye to making the pilgrimage routes safe again, Pope Urban II issued a call for a crusade at the Council of Clermont in 1095. Kings, noblemen, knights, and their retainers flocked to the cause, promised full forgiveness of all their sins if they made the crusade to liberate the Holy City from the hands of the Saracens.

United under the banner of the cross, Christian armies swept across the Levant and in 1099 managed to conquer the Saracens and take the Holy City. But their victory was temporary; battles for Jerusalem and the neighboring region continued to be fought for several centuries. European noblemen established domains and principalities in the Middle East, which they and their descendants occupied for two hundred years before being convincingly ousted in 1291. Constantinople, with its unique Eastern Orthodox Christian heritage, was the capitol of the Byzantine Empire. It was also a thriving metropolis that had provided a beacon of civilization throughout the period when the Dark Ages held western Europe in their grip. Following the crusades, the cross-fertilization of the Byzantine and Islamic civilizations of the East bore fruit in increased trade, building enterprises, and cultural achievements in the West. Encountering the wealth and highly civilized cities of medieval Byzantium and Islam, the relatively crude and primitive westerners were inspired to implement fresh ideas in architecture, art, and quality of living. This fortuitous contact with the luxuries of the East seems to have sparked an early renaissance in southern Europe during the twelfth century that was, sadly, nipped in the bud by the brutally repressive Inquisition formed in the thirteenth.

Perhaps it was their encounter with the searing heat of the deserts of the Near East that inspired the returning Crusaders to build temples in Europe to honor Our Lady. Whatever the reason, the twelfth century witnessed a remarkable burst of construction. The mathematics and science of the Arab world helped western architects and engineers to design and construct the soaring arches of the Gothic style into these cathedrals dedicated to the Queen of Heaven. Laid out on the ground across the center of France, the sites of the new temples formed an image of the constellation Virgo on the ground, a mirror of the heavens and reminder of the adage: As above, so below. Money was invested, blueprints were submitted, and masons and artisans were employed. Europe blossomed in a fever of activity; whole towns were involved in the project, even the nobles doing manual labor in some cases alongside the stonecutters and carpenters.

Day by day, the walls of the cathedrals grew taller, the economy grew stronger, the merchants grew more affluent. "Our Lady" was pleased. Townsfolk and local nobility abandoned their feuding and concentrated on building their fabulous structures in her honor, constructing the beautiful Gothic churches and abbeys still visited by throngs of pilgrims. Artists and artisans, those carriers of culture and civilization, were fully employed with carving, sculpting, painting, and molding the great themes of Christianity to decorate the new palaces built in honor of the "Lady of France." The sacred geometry of the ancient world was at the heart of the new style, and it is rumored that the masons and the Knights of the Temple of Solomon, whose money was heavily invested in the building of these new temples, built the tenets of the true faith into the stones and structures of the churches. If this is so, then it is the graceful stones of the arches themselves that proclaim the true faith, for Gothic arches form the geometric symbol associated with the feminine principle as the "doorway of life" and the "Holy of Holies"—the *Vesica Piscis*.

The cathedrals of the twelfth century mirror the philosophy and worldview of their builders and architects: the Feminine was being honored in an unprecedented fashion, proclaimed Queen of Heaven, Mother of All, and Eternal Bride. The coronation of Our Lady in heaven became a frequent subject for artists. This apotheosis of the Feminine manifests itself most obviously perhaps in the stunning, even miraculous, creations of stained glass that are the glory of Our Lady's temples, especially in France. Carefully cut shards of glass shine like jewels, the intricate mosaics forming glowing images of incredible beauty. The formulas for creating the dyes used to color the glass were a closely guarded secret of the artisans, probably derived from artisans in the Middle East; the effect of their chemistry, the gem-like quality of their fragments, is sublimely manifest in the rose window of Chartres Cathedral, as well as a thousand other windows of medieval churches. The stonecutters and sculptors carved the themes of Christianity into the structures; the artificers in glass recreated the Gospel stories and parables in their mosaics. The entire cathedral became a visual symphony to honor and to celebrate the eternal Queen of Earth and Heaven.

The awesome towers were finally in place, and their bells began to chime all over Europe, beckoning people to prayer and to community: to lauds, to matins, to vespers and to compline, ringing out the canonical hours of the Divine Office. Townspeople came to worship, pilgrims gathered, and bishops of the Roman Catholic Church presided over the towns and surrounding villages of their dioceses. To the casual observer, Christianity was enjoying the splendid apex of its unity under one creed, one faith, and one Holy Father in Rome, the vicar of Christ on earth. But underneath the new structures raised on ancient holy sites, springs of the Sacred Feminine still burbled, the waters of spirit and truth from the underground streams of prophecy welling up to nurture the spiritual life of the people.

European Sites of Pilgrimage

Second only to Jerusalem as a pilgrimage site was Rome itself. Her marble pillars and beautiful arches and plazas were a reminder of the pinnacle of worldly power to which Rome's emperors had aspired, although the pope now ruled the imperial city. Rome was more accessible than Jerusalem, by far, but her sites were made sacred, not by the footsteps of Jesus, but rather by those of his apostles Peter and Paul—the ostensible founders of the Christian Church of Rome.

Another pilgrimage site rivaled Rome for popularity—the site of Santiago de Compostela, believed to have been the final resting place of James, the brother of Jesus who had been the leader of the early Christian community in Jerusalem. Shod in sandals, staff in hand, sporting the scallop shell as their badge, the faithful of western Europe crisscrossed their way along the old pilgrimage routes to this holy shrine. The city was believed to have been a center of the purest and most legitimate Christian teaching—that of the brother of Jesus, whose bones are said to have been brought there for burial from Jerusalem where he suffered his martyrdom, thrown down from the wall of the Temple.

A fourth favorite site of pilgrimage for medieval devotees was the Basilica of Mary Magdalene at Vézelay in the very heart of France. The second crusade was preached in 1140 by Saint Bernard of Clairvaux himself from the steps of this famous Romanesque abbey. Aflame with the rhetoric of the saintly Bernard, Eleanor of Aquitaine, the queen of the French king, Louis VII, heard the appeal and, after assembling an enormous entourage of servants and retainers, insisted on accompanying her husband on his crusade to the Holy Land.

The bones of Mary Magdalene, the beloved saint who walked with Jesus during his ministry and met him resurrected on Easter morning, were rediscovered in 1280 in an obscure tomb in Provence, kept secret during the extended period of the Moors' occupation of the Mediterranean coast of France. These sacred relics were later transported to her basilica, "La Madeleine," at Vézelay for safekeeping, although her skull, complete with reddish blonde hair, remained at her cathedral at Saint Maximin. Legends of Mary Magdalene and her presence in France were immensely popular, and pilgrims flocked to Vézelay, many climbing the town's hill barefoot to reach the grand Romanesque abbey church at its summit. Others thronged to Saintes-Maries-de-la-Mer to honor her, or to Sainte Baume, the grotto where she was believed to have spent the last thirty years of her life as a hermit recluse, clothed in her own hair. So much merit was attached to the practice of pilgrimage and to the viewing and touching of holy relics of the saints, that the claims to the authenticity and preeminence of these sacramentals grew steadily out of control, with European cities competing for the honor of having the most significant and holy relics in their possession.

Among the most popular sites of pilgrimage in Britain is Glastonbury, the home of the earliest Christians in Britain. Saint Joseph of Arimathea, the friend of Jesus who buried him in the tomb in his garden, is believed to have brought a small group of Christian refugees to this remote corner of the Roman Empire, where they were given sufficient land by the Briton king Arviragus to build a small village of huts. The family and disciples of Joseph are credited with building the country's earliest Christian church at Glastonbury. The spring they found there supplied their water needs and is now "Glastonbury Well," renowned for its healing properties. It was here that Joseph planted his staff, which sprouted and grew into the "Holy Thorn" that blooms at Christmas time, and it is to Glastonbury that he is said to have brought the chalice from which Jesus drank at the Last

The Glastonbury Well is a place of beauty and peace. It is also a place of healing. Spiritual pilgrims of all kinds have come to this special place. The earliest Christian church was believed to have been built at Glastonbury.

Supper, although this legend appears to have started rather late in connection with Glastonbury, probably in the twelfth century, about the time the other legends about the Grail were appearing in literary form on the continent.

Pilgrimages to the Black Madonna

This Wayside Madonna by artist Edith Catlin Phelps, painted in 1939, reminds us of the renowned and intriguing representations of the Black Madonna that were common throughout Europe in the Middle Ages.

One of the greatest enigmas of religious history in the Middle Ages is the popular fascination with the image of the Black Madonna. The very first crusade to liberate the Holy Land was preached from Clermont, a town in central France distinguished by its cathedral. There, behind the main altar, is a famous representation of the Black Madonna enthroned in majesty, a tenth-century Romanesque statue of a woman garbed entirely in gold and holding her son on her lap. The faces and hands of both mother and child are ebony—deliberately and irrevocably black. There is no possible suggestion here that they might have been discolored by candle smoke or soot or age, as perennially suggested by local clergy attempting to explain the anomaly. The Madonna and her son are black. This statue, like many others in southern Europe, was highly celebrated with a medieval festival and pilgrimage from a very early date.

The dark face of the Madonna is an enigma in medieval Europe that continues to intrigue Christians and inspire them to pilgrimage. Her effigy occurs in numerous shrines in western Europe, and pilgrims flocked to popular shrines of the Madonna, most often holding the Divine Child on her lap—a pose already familiar in traditional statues and paintings of the Virgin Mary holding Jesus. Medieval devotees probably would not have known that similar statues depicted the Egyptian goddess Isis and her son Horus; they merely assumed that the dark lady was their

Another popular site of pilgrimage in England is Canterbury, where the Archbishop Thomas à Becket was murdered by the minions of King Henry II, who was outraged by his former friend's intense loyalty to the Church at the expense of the power of the crown. Thomas was immediately canonized in the hearts of the people who flocked to the cathedral to pay homage to their saintly hero.

Blessed Virgin, the Mother of God. Her darkness was widely assumed to be due to her Middle Eastern blood, although in Clermont-Ferrand, Marseilles, and Einsiedeln, Our Lady is jet black. The image housed at the Cathedral of Notre Dame of Clermont was hidden away during some long-forgotten period of danger; she was sealed up in the walls of the cathedral, where she remained safely hidden from view until renovations of the building revealed her hiding place in 1974. Like the Sacred Feminine she embodies, she has been in protective custody, hidden away and forgotten, for centuries—an interesting synchronicity! It was clearly time for her unveiling, corresponding with movements for the liberation of women worldwide.

Pilgrims walked, often barefoot, the long miles from shrine to shrine, seeking favors of the Madonna, who was known to bless the barren womb and heal unhappy marriages. Mercy was the trademark of the Madonna, and her motherly concern for her children was boundless. One of her most popular and venerated shrines is located in the lady chapel of the fantastic French town of Rocamadour, literally built into the hillside. Here her slim, almost emaciated, wooden replica is silver-plated, blackened by tarnish. Among other famous supplicants, Saint Louis, Saint Bernard, and Eleanor of Aquitaine visited Our Lady of Rocamadour. She was renowned for her compassionate intercession in severe cases of infertility, imprisonment, and dangers at sea. Metal shackles shed by former prisoners are heaped in gratitude at her feet. The lame abandoned their crutches at Rocamadour—as they still do in many of the numerous shrines and chapels of the Dark Lady in Europe's medieval churches. Large numbers of votive candles were lit in supplication for her favor and compassion. Among her legends is a charming story that she revived a stillborn infant so it could live long enough to be baptized, thus sparing it the pain and ignominy of spending eternal life in limbo, and instead bringing it directly to heaven. This is very typical of the renowned compassion of the Black Virgin who waives the rules of the institution and responds to the pleas of the faithful with her heart. It is not at the feet of Saint Peter that votive candles are universally lit, but at the feet of Our Lady.

Another highly revered Black Madonna is housed in the fifth-century crypt of the Basilica of Saint Victor, high over the harbor in Marseilles. This abbey church was built by Saint John Cassian for his double monastery of monks and nuns, and the crypt contains catacombs and the well of Saint Blaise. Here the Madonna is called "Our Lady of the Witness" (*Notre Dame de la Confession*) and "Our Lady of New Fire" (*Notre Dame de Feu-Nou*), a reference to her preeminent feast at this site, the feast of Candlemas. This traditional "purification

> *I am as black—but lovely—as the tents of Kedar . . .*
> *Do not stare at me because I am swarthy, because the sun has burned me.*
> *My brothers have been angry with me. They charged me with the care of their vineyards. My own vineyard I have not kept.*
> (SONG OF SONGS 1.5–6)

of Our Lady" on February 2 coincides with the ancient feast day of Imbolc, when the chaff from the previous year's harvest was burnt off so that the fields would be purified for the spring replanting. Long before Christian times, Marseilles also honored Isis, the "Queen of Heaven and Earth," who traveled across the world searching for her lost consort, Osiris. On the feast of Candlemas, Marseilles honors Mary Magdalene and the "other Marys" who, according to legend, voyaged to the coast of Gaul in a tiny boat with no oars, bringing with them the Gospel of the risen Christ.

Little cakes called *navettes* are baked for this feast day of the Black Madonna, whose effigy is carried out of her crypt and through the streets by an escort of city dignitaries and church officials in a candle-lit procession. The cakes are very distinctive, little rectangles with a small slit down the center, which, when the dough rises, forms a distinct "*Vesica Piscis*" resembling a little canoe— the "bark of Isis" and that of the three refugee Marys. Here the conflation of the Mother of Jesus, the Magdalene, and the Black Madonna is almost palpable. Which Mary brought the Gospel to Marseille and witnessed there to the "Good News" of the risen Christ? Their legend in France insists that there were three!

This () shape formed when two circles intersect is fundamental in sacred geometry, where it is called the "matrix" or "mother" of all other geometric shapes; it is also the shape associated with the Feminine, the "womb" and the "doorway to life." By gematria, which is an ancient system that gives numerical value to the letters of the Greek alphabet, the *Vesica Piscis* is associated with the name Maria (152) and, even more conclusively, with the epithet "the Magadalene" (153) found in the Gospels.[12] The Cathedral of Notre Dame in Paris is actually built on an island in the Seine that has the same () shape—the Île de Paris is the "bark of Our Lady." The earliest Christian Church on this sacred site was built to honor Magdalene and bore her name.

Our Lady at Chartres

The cathedral at Chartres has the distinction of housing two famous Black Virgin statues. One of the oldest dark Madonnas resided in the crypt of the great Gothic edifice built to honor her at Chartres. The same site once marked the capital city of the Druids, and legend maintains that an ancient statue of the "Lady about to give birth" was housed at Chartres long before Christianity arrived in Gaul. The original statue of the serene and majestic dark Virgin seated on her throne, "Our Lady of the Underground" (*Notre Dame de Sous-Terre*), was destroyed during the French Revolution but replaced in 1856 using an old carved replica as a model.

Near the statue of Our Lady's in the ancient crypt is "the Well of the Strong," renowned as a healing spring that was reputedly a popular site of Druid pilgrimage. Christianity often incorporated existing shrines of pagan forebears into its churches and sacred places, and ancient springs were universally sacred to the earth or mother goddess. Remove your shoes when you enter here, for this is holy ground!

Our Lady of Czestochowa

Veneration of the Black Madonna was not confined to France. One of the most famous icons is the scarred visage of Our Lady of Czestochowa in Poland, which legend claims was painted by Saint Luke, although a slightly more plausible theory is that it was painted in Carolingian France and taken to the Balkans by the armies of Charlemagne. From there, the painting was likely carried to Poland as part of the dowry of a Byzantine princess in 1382. It is housed in the Monastery of Jasna Gora, "mountain of light." No one can say how her image became scarred; some have suggested that her painted cheek was scratched and desecrated by robbers who attacked the monastery. Uncannily (or perhaps by design?), a line in the prophecy of Micah speaks of the bruised cheek of the Daughter of Sion, Ruler of Israel (Micah 4.14).

Our Lady of Czestochowa is the patroness of Poland and is credited with many powerful miracles, including the defeat of the Swedish army of Gustavus Adolphus, which took place during the Thirty Years War (1618–1648). More recently, her intercession is recognized in the victory of the Polish Solidarity movement over the Communist regime, eventually leading to the 1989 fall of the Berlin Wall and the dissolution of the Soviet Union. Our Lady is a powerful advocate on behalf of freedom

Displayed at Jasna Gora in Poland, the Black Madonna of Czestochowa is the patroness of the Polish people in their struggle for freedom from foreign hegemony, which has lasted for centuries.

fighters and the *anawim*, the "little ones of God." The Madonna with the dark visage can be found at the vanguard of liberation movements worldwide: those seeking to release women from shackles of inequality and repression and those seeking equality and justice for the oppressed and abused. She hears the cry of the poor.

Our Lady of Guadalupe

Not confining the realm of her jurisdiction to Europe, Our Lady's dark image was miraculously imprinted into the cloak of a simple peasant in Mexico soon after Spanish conquistadors conquered his people and converted them to the faith they carried to the New World. In 1531, the lovely Lady revealed herself to Juan Diego and requested that a chapel be built to her as "merciful mother" on a mountainside that had previously been honored by the indigenous tribes as sacred to their own mother goddess. The Lady instructed Juan to gather roses on the nearby hillside and wrap them in his cloak, which he must then take to the bishop with a request to build a chapel to Our Lady on the site. When he opened his mantle to show the flowers to the Spanish bishop, the miraculous image of "Our Lady of Guadalupe" appeared in the coarsely woven cloak. The bishop found the extravagant display of fragrant fresh roses all the more convincing because the miracle occurred in mid-December. The dark-faced Madonna resembles the Mexican natives who make pilgrimages to her, often climbing the cathedral hill of Guadalupe on their knees. The image imprinted in Juan's mantle is that of the Cosmic Mother, standing on the moon, dressed in rich floral brocade, and clothed in a blue cloak representing the star-studded midnight sky. The baby Jesus does not accompany his mother at Guadalupe; Our Lady stands alone in majesty— Our Lady of the Roses. She has been adopted as the patron of the unborn and of the anti-abortion movement among Roman Catholic activists in the United States. She has also been designated the "patroness of the Americas" by the Roman Catholic Church.

The Virgin of Guadalupe, "clothed with the sun, with the moon under her feet," is described in Revelation 12. Her miraculous image was imprinted in the cloak of an indigenous Mexican peasant in 1531. Our Lady of Guadalupe is "Patroness of the Americas."

Our Lady of Clearwater

At Christmastime, in 1996, the dark Madonna revealed her face once again, this time in a sun-splashed suburb of St. Petersburg, Florida, in a town called Clearwater. Officially, the spontaneous appearance of the eloquent image was formed by the impact of water from a sprinkler system against the window of a financial building, which caused a chemical reaction in the glass. The timing was, however, particularly powerful. The Tampa Bay area had been experiencing heightened racial tensions during the preceding weeks. With the "miraculous" appearance of the Madonna—not in "Peter's town" let it be noted, but in its adjacent suburb "Clearwater"—brought a tide of compassion and reconciliation to the heated disputes. The parking lot of the financial building whose window held the image of "Our Lady of Clearwater" quickly became a shrine and a place of pilgrimage for thousands of visitors who flock there still, carrying flowers or candles which they light at the base of the building. This amazing synchronicity underlines the symbolic value of the underground stream and the waters of spirit and truth often associated with the Sacred Feminine.

Who is the Dark Lady and why is she black? Among the ancient peoples, earth and moon goddesses (Artemis, Cybele, and Isis) were often black, as equal opposites/counterparts of the sun god. Christians, encountering images of such goddesses from the past, may simply have copied them, especially those of Isis with Horus on her lap. Another suggested reason for the blackness of the Madonna images is found in the Hebrew Book of Lamentations 4:8: "The princes of Judah whose faces were once white as milk are now black as soot; they are not recognized in the streets." It is possible that the dark visage of the Madonna and her child are in reference to the widow of Sion and the royal bloodline of Judah, the line of King David. It is this claim of "sangraal" (blood royal) that lies at the heart of the Grail heresy of medieval Europe. Alternatively, the Queen of the South, Sheba, is often associated with Wisdom/Sophia, the Bride of Solomon, and she, like the dark Shulamite in the Song of Songs, is black. Perhaps she represents Holy Wisdom personified as a woman.

In addition to these theories, there is a poignant line from the Hebrew Bible's Song of Songs (the Song of Solomon) that declares that the Bride is black, swarthy from her labor in her brothers' vineyards. This line sums up the global condition of the Sacred Feminine principle, burned out in menial service to the ascendant Masculine principle all across the planet. Her face sunburned and even scarred, like that of the Polish Madonna, the Dark Lady represents the devalued and denigrated "Bride." It is the people who image the Feminine Face of God, they who mirror the unseen Holy One. This condition of the "Bride"—representative of the "little poor ones"—is summed up in the scarred visage of the Black Madonna so devoutly revered for her infinite mercy.

> *Now I, like a rivulet from her stream, channeling the waters into a garden, said to myself, "I will water my plants, my flower bed I will drench."*
> (SIRACH 24.28–29)

PRACTICE:
LABYRINTH MEDITATION

The traditional labyrinth is an intricate spiral pattern of great antiquity. It first appears in the classical myth of Ariadne, who helped the Athenean hero Theseus slay the Minotaur in the labyrinth of Knossos in Crete. The interior path of the maze is a symbol for the journey of the soul. Walking a labyrinth with deliberation and intention is a spiritual practice similar to silent meditation, leading one deep into the center of one's being where the Divine is encountered. In medieval times, to walk the labyrinth was a peasant's substitute for a pilgrimage to Jerusalem, a journey that was prohibitively expensive for the poor. The pattern was usually walked barefoot and with a special spiritual intention or prayer of intercession expressed at the beginning of the walk. The classic labyrinth does not have dead ends, but always leads to the center and then back to the starting point—symbolic of the Holy Spirit who faithfully guides and never abandons the pilgrim soul, bringing it safely home.

The traditional labyrinth is sometimes laid out in the stone floor of a church, as in the Cathedral of Notre Dame in Chartres, or, more often in modern times, on a level site in a woods or meadow. A lovely outdoor labyrinth can easily be laid out. The size of the pattern can be adapted to the size of the garden, but typically the circle should be at least twenty feet in diameter. A special shrub or tree may be chosen to grace the center of the pattern. A small bench might also be placed in this center space, for continuing meditation. Another delightful enhancement could be a small fountain representing the nurturing waters of the Holy Spirit, or perhaps a little bird bath. The stone labyrinth in the floor of Chartres Cathedral has a six-petal flower in the center, where pilgrims kneel to pray before beginning their return journey.

Lay the paths out carefully according to the pattern illustrated on page 73. Some labyrinths are laid out by lining the path with small rocks. Others use gravel or tiny white pebbles to form the actual paths, with flowers planted between them. One of the most delightful labyrinths I ever walked was laid out in curved rows of vegetables; another was done with rows of fragrant herbs. Typically the paths to be walked are about a foot wide. The number of rows will depend on the diameter of the sacred space you are able to devote to the project. With slightly more effort, a labyrinth can be laid out in a wooded area, allowing slight variations in the pattern to accommodate existing trees. This extra challenge is rewarded by the peace and protection of the sylvan canopy.

Whether you build your own outdoor labyrinth, walk an existing one, or use your finger to trace the labyrinth pattern provided here, this ancient symbol can have a powerful meditative effect. As you walk, you may wish to hold in mind a prayer for intercession or recite a familiar prayer such as the "Ave Maria" or "Memorare." Because of the very personal nature of meditation, many people find that the prayer of their own heart arises spontaneously as they walk. Here is an example of a simple prayer you can use for your walk:

Spirit of the Living God, be my guide and
traveling companion as I walk the spiritual path.
Lead me gently into the depths of my being.
Enlighten and reveal to me anything that
hinders me on my journey into mature spirituality.
Help me to experience the profound peace
and mystery of the indwelling Divine.

When you reach the center of the labyrinth, you may wish to rest quietly for some minutes. Then, on the return journey out of the labyrinth, allow a prayer like the following to arise:

As I return now to the world, a pilgrim soul born
of God and of earth, bestow on me the gift of
living gracefully and in gentle harmony with all
whom I encounter and with all creation. Help me
to carry the mystery of the Divine Presence into
all aspects of my daily life.

This intricate thirteenth-century labyrinth in the floor of Chartres Cathedral, with its closed pattern of curves, provides a pattern for the inner journey.

CHAPTER FIVE

THE ROSE IN BLOOM

Arise my beloved, my fair one, and come!

For winter is over and done . . .

the flowers appear on the earth . . .

the song of the dove is heard in our land.

(SONG OF SONGS 2.10–12)

The Rose in Bloom

When the Lady instructed Juan Diego to gather flowers in his mantle, she caused roses to bloom out of season, for the rose is the most ancient symbol of the Divine Feminine. This most fragrant and exotic flower with velvet petals of crimson, white, or pink was sacred to Aphrodite/Venus in the classical world. The word *rose* is an anagram for *Eros*, the principle of erotic love and relationship. Somehow, that connection does not appear to be accidental. In Christian symbolism, roses, both red and white, are often associated with the Virgin Mary, the carrier of the feminine aspects of the Divine. The cultural resurgence of Europe under her aegis was remarkable. In the wake of the Crusades and the building of cathedrals and towns that followed, the standard of living rose steadily in Europe. Arts and crafts flourished in the towns that sprang into existence almost overnight. Displayed at the apex of this activity were the resplendent mosaic "rose" windows of the cathedrals of Our Lady, sparkling with jewel-like intensity in the sunlight. The "voice of the Bride" was again heard in the land, and her songs seemed to be wafting on the breeze, coming like the trill and warble of the nightingale from the woods and meadows of Provence. Europe was hearing a new song.

Saint Bernard's vision of the Virgin Mary inspired fervent devotion to the Blessed Mother in medieval Europe.

Jesu!—the very thought is sweet!
In that dear name all heart-joys meet;
But sweeter than the honey far
The glimpses of his presence are.
(FROM "THE ROSY SEQUENCE," BERNARD OF
CLAIRVAUX (?), TR. JOHN MASON NEALE[13])

At the same time, in the heart of the twelfth century, the idea of Christ as eternal heavenly Bridegroom enjoyed a resurrection. In his *Commentary* on the Song of Songs, a series of eighty-six sermons given for brother monks of his Cistercian order, Saint Bernard of Clairvaux spiritualized Eros, presenting Jesus as a gentle lover of each Christian. The ardent soul, Bernard noted, is personified by Mary of Bethany sitting at the feet of Jesus, devotedly attentive to his teachings. In his series of sermons, Bernard spoke at length about the tender care lavished by Christ on his "beloved"—the soul—and of her devotion to her sweet Lord. This language of love—erotic love even—of Saint Bernard's sermons revolutionized the contemporary view of Jesus as Victor, Ruler, and Judge, and replaced him with a sweet and loving Savior, ardent in his desire for intimate relationship with each soul. This kinder and gentler Jesus surprised the hierarchical clergy and the established monastic orders that emphasized ascetic practice and strict discipline. The face of Christianity softened.

The Cathars' Church of Love

But in the midst of this cultural resurgence of the Feminine principle, it was perceived that all was not well. A new, unauthorized song reached the ears of the bishops arrayed in brocade vestments and seated in the intricately carved and gilded thrones of their newly built cathedrals, and they shuddered. The saintly Bernard of Clairvaux was dispatched to investigate the strange melodies coming from the south—the unacceptable tenets of a virulent heresy that was gradually spreading northward from its cradle in Provence.

"No sermons are more Christian than theirs," Bernard reported, "and their morals are pure." He was speaking of the Cathars, a sect of Christians declared heretical by the hierarchy of the Roman Catholic Church. This is high praise indeed from one of the foremost prelates in France, speaking about heretics who were deemed anti-clerical and anti-ecclesiastic, and who disdained the sacraments and liturgies of the Roman tradition, preaching instead a life of humble simplicity, enlightened faith, and personal responsibility. These converts to the alternative Christian Way of Love repudiated the cross as a brutal Roman instrument of

Ruins of Cathar citadels like this one crown numerous summits in the region of Aude in southern France.

torture and embraced instead the "song of the dove"—the direct guidance of the Holy Spirit in their lives— relying on the saving power of enlightenment through personal encounter with the Divine rather than the blood sacrifice of Jesus. For Cathars, Christianity was not a creed to be memorized, but rather, a faith to be lived, following the example of Christ: essentially characterized by humble service and solidarity with the poor.

From Christianity's inception, its followers had developed many alternative or "heterodox" views, but most of them had been efficiently and effectively squelched over the centuries. The Cathars derived much of their doctrine from a heresy that had sprung up among eleventh-century peasants in

A representation of Courtly Love, where a "Lady" (Dompna) becomes an idealized figure who inspires a knight to lofty goals and heroism.

were living the Christian principles of voluntary simplicity, love of neighbor, and generous service to the poor. Theirs was a Church of Love (*Amor*), an anagram of the Church of "Roma," whose priests and prelates they perceived as living a corrupt and legalistic perversion of the true Gospel. The Cathars believed their doctrines to be of purer origin and greater authenticity than those of Rome. They maintained that theirs was a church based on the original Gospel teachings of Jesus—pure and uncorrupted, a church based on personal enlightenment rather than indoctrination. They called themselves Christians.

the Balkans and that by the mid-twelfth century had spread westward across Lombardy and into France. The doctrines of the sect seem to be dualistic, derived from those of third-century Manicheism, and became a synthesis of Gnostic and Zoroastrian thought and practice.

But it was not its dualist doctrines that made the Cathar heresy so dangerous. Rather, it was its basis in the Gospels and the sincerity, integrity, and noble character of its ministers, which caused it to spread like wildfire. The *Cathari*, "the pure ones," traveled in pairs throughout southern Europe, preaching the Gospel of Jesus to those laboring in fields and orchards, working side-by-side with them and sharing their meager fare. In a period when the clergy of the established Church were becoming venal, lax, and even corpulent, the ascetic and charismatic "pure ones" of the Cathars

Papermills sprang up in southern France to provide paper for the great project of the Cathars—to provide the Gospels in the vernacular to the adherents of their faith. These precursors of the Protestant Reformation distinguished themselves by translating the Vulgate (Latin Scriptures) and making them available to the faithful of their sect. Often their favorite Gospel, that of John, was worn on a cord under their clothes. Fossils of their forgotten faith in the form of watermarks are found ingeniously imbedded in the actual leaves of paper found in their bibles. Because "enlightenment" and "walking in the light" were the foundation doctrines of their faith, it is symbolically fitting that their emblems are only visible when the page into which they were secretly manufactured is held up to the light. The earliest watermarks seem to date from 1280, and the practice continued throughout the years of the Protestant Reformation of the sixteenth century, providing evidence that their alternative Christianity survived underground in spite of the "dungeon, fire, and sword" unleashed upon it by the Church of Rome.

In a significant departure from the orthodox practice, both boys and girls were taught to read. Many converts to this "pure" Christianity were wealthy women, who provided the alternative Church with financial support. Among the Cathars, women were accepted as ministers. Garbed in dark blue robes, they traveled in pairs throughout the region, just as the male evangelists of their faith did, in contrast to the Roman Church, which had concretized the words of Paul's Epistle to Timothy: "I do not allow a woman to teach" (1 Tim. 2.12). What the Cathars actually taught is not fully known, because in 1209 the pope and the French king launched a crusade against these "Albigensian heretics," and in 1237, the Inquisition was formed to destroy what remained of the dissident sects. Their documents and books were confiscated and burned, destroying most of the evidence, and they were accused of various blasphemies and false teachings, many of which seem to have been misunderstood by the Inquisitors. But the pure morals and high idealism of the sectarians, coupled with the relatively independent spirit of the region's inhabitants, ensured the continued spread of their faith in the "underground stream" of prophetic utterance that surfaced again during the Reformation several hundred years later.

Courtly Love

Concurrent with the Albigensian heresies in the twelfth and thirteenth centuries in southern France, we encounter another related anomaly—the exotic blossoming of the culture of the troubadour and the spread of the ideals of courtly love. The songs of this period, written and sung in the vernacular of the *langue d'oc*, celebrated the beauty of the land, the spring, the lush green forests and meadows with their colorful carpets of wild flowers, and the tender emotions of erotic love. Often these feelings are addressed to a "Beloved," called the *Dompna*, which is the Provençal word for the Latin word *Domina*, the "Lady," the one whom the poet would serve forever, wanting only to please her. In most cases, she is not his wife, nor even his sweetheart. She is far removed, an idealized feminine who inspires him to lofty goals and even to heroism. Under the civilizing influence of this resurgent honor of the Feminine, the knights and noblemen of the Middle Ages began to clean up their behavior, combed their hair, washed their faces, and aspired to compose poetry and play the zither.

Why cry not all, out of their sorrow deep, To Heaven, and ask how long the Lord will sleep? . . . His treasurer steals the hoard of grace given in his care; His peace-maker plunders here and murders there; His shepherd has become a wolf among His sheep.

(INNOCENT III, WALTHER VON DER VOGELWEIDE, GERMAN MINNESINGER, FL. 1198–1228, TR. JETHRO BITHELL[14])

Troubadours were not confined to France but traveled throughout Europe, where the phenomena of "courtly love" and the "courteous knight" sprang up in their wake, experienced in the call of the nightingale, the bud on the vine, the blush on the cheek of the beloved. This renewal seems to be a reaction against the austerity and strict discipline of the Roman Church—as if Lent had lasted too long! Suddenly the way of the heart burst forth in exultant refrains, celebrating the goodness of the earth and the beauty of the "Lady," and spawning a Renaissance from the attitudes and mores of the Dark Ages.

From the citadels of southern France, many of which were Cathar strongholds and seminaries for their alternative faith, the cult of courtly love spread north, spawning the related songs and culture of the German *minnesingers*—the singers who praised the Lady and her sweet love.

Praised be my Lord God with all His creatures, and especially our brother the sun, who brings us the day and who brings us the light; fair is he . . . Praised be my Lord for our sister the moon, and for the stars the which He has set clear and lovely in heaven . . .
(Song of the Creatures, Saint Francis of Assisi, tr. Matthew Arnold[15])

It was she who enlightened and inspired their songs, she whom they delighted in serving, she whose wish was their command. It has been suggested that many of the songs extolling the virtues and inspiration of the *Dompna* were actually written to honor the Cathar faith, the personified "true love" of the troubadour, whose desires and admonitions he lived to fulfill.[16] The poetry of the troubadours is rife with puns, metaphors, and biblical as well as classical references. It is replete with double meanings that could easily be hiding secret references to the "other Church"—the Church of Amor. The singer adores his mistress; he cannot resist singing her praises and wishes to serve her in all things. She is his inspiration for taking the crusader's cross and he holds her in honor, although her name is kept in secret. She is above all the most beautiful, most desirable, most cherished.

Because an obscure tenet of Gnosticism was the intimate partnership of Jesus and Mary Magdalene, it seems possible that the *Dompna* was, at least for some of their poets, the sweet Lady of their Lord: she was the Christian "goddess" denied and scorned by the Roman hierarchy—the Mary called "the Magdalene."

In 1277, the troubadours' songs were declared heretical—that is, having religious content found to be at variance with the doctrines and traditions of the Roman Catholic Church. Many were forced into exile, their voices permanently silenced, while some merely changed their tune and wrote poems and songs honoring the Virgin as their "Lady."

Saint Francis

One of the most beloved of all Christianity's saints, who abandoned all things for the love of Christ, called himself a "troubadour of God." Saint Francis di Bernardone (1181–1226) was born to a wealthy fabric merchant in the Tuscan town of Assisi. Scholars speculate that his mother was a Cathar; in any case, she was from Provence and no doubt influenced by its prevailing culture. The poetry of Saint Francis reflects the tradition of those who saw God manifested in creation and loved the earth and her creatures. Francis felt the kinship of all creation taught by mystics of all ages: He called the sun and wind our brothers, the moon our sister. Animals and birds were also our kin. Like Hildegard of Bingen, this gentle saint has the distinction of being one of the earliest environmentalists in history.

The teachings of Saint Francis have many correspondences with what is known about the Cathars. He modeled his mendicant friars on the Cathar missionaries of the region, embracing poverty and chastity, traveling in pairs, and sharing their bread with the workers in the fields. People yearned for justice, peace, and freedom, virtues explicit in the Gospel teachings of Jesus, and they recognized them in the practice of the Cathars and the simple brown-robed Franciscan friars. One of a later generation of Franciscan friars is said to have remarked: "If Jesus walked, why do bishops ride?"

Saint Francis was not always a saint. His playboy youth was wild and misspent. He joined an army of mercenaries as a young man and was badly wounded in battle, narrowly escaping with his life. His mother nursed him back to health, but before he could resume his dissolute lifestyle and return to his military duties, he had a conversion experience. One Sunday, during the celebration of the Mass, Francis saw the figure of Jesus on the crucifix above the altar crying. He began receiving locutions and was asked by Jesus to "rebuild my Church." So Francis went out to a neighboring

Giotto's familiar fresco of Francis of Assisi, with one of his friars, depicts the saint preaching to the birds, which he regarded, together with animals, as kin to humanity.

valley and began to rebuild an old church that had fallen into ruins. Drawn by the charisma of Francis, many of his old friends and cohorts gathered to assist in this work, and the group gradually grew in size, in grace, and in renown, eventually developing into a community rebuilding the little church.

Francis soon realized that he needed an organizing principle for this infant community, so he deliberately opened the Bible to see what instruction he would receive from God. First, he read the command of Jesus given to the rich young man to sell all his goods and give to the poor. When he opened his Bible the second time, he found the order to the apostles to take nothing on their journey, and the third time, he encountered the demand to take up the cross daily. Francis was convinced that these exhortations were the basis of the rule that Jesus intended for him to follow with his friends. They began their missionary work, bringing the Gospels to the people, just as their neighboring Cathars had been doing for decades.

Amusing stories are told of Saint Francis. Once, when a robber stole the hood of one of the brothers, Francis made the friar offer the robber his robe as well. He was a friend to all creatures, believing that God delighted in his birds and animals and that all of creation was interrelated in kinship. A book called *The Little Flowers of Saint Francis* contains the famous story of his encounter with a predatory wolf that was intimidating the townspeople of Gubbio. This wolf was very dangerous and had been attacking people as well as their domestic animals. But, making the sign of the cross, Saint Francis approached the wolf and spoke gently to him, addressing him as "Brother Wolf," and the beast lay down at his feet like a docile lamb. Saint Francis then persuaded the wolf to cease preying on the town and promised in return that the people would give him all the food he needed. When the wolf agreed, the compact was made. The people rejoiced at their liberation and happily fed the wolf for the rest of his days! Perhaps this incident was what inspired Saint Francis to create the first creche and to include an image of a wolf in the group of animals that flanked the Holy Family during the Nativity.

Saint Clare

Not all of the followers of Saint Francis were men. Saint Clare (1194–1253), like Francis, was also born in Assisi, the daughter of well-to-do parents. As a young child she knew of Francis and his community of brothers and was drawn to them, over the objections of her parents, becoming a nun and persuading Francis to help her found her own order, the Poor Sisters of Clare, as a sister community to his friars. The film *Brother Sun, Sister Moon*, the story of Saint Francis, has a charming scene in which Saint Francis cuts Clare's hair before she takes her vows. No doubt this is an exaggeration, but it expresses very poignantly the mutual devotion of the pair to one another and to God. Like many medieval clergy and religious, Clare practiced severe asceticism, living for years on the border of starvation and damaging her health in the process. She was renowned for her holiness and the cures wrought by her intercession, as well as for the chaste but passionate love she shared with Francis.

Delightful stories are told of Clare in *The Little Flowers of Saint Francis*, which calls her one of the sweetest of his flowers. Clare was so holy that even the pope came to visit her often. One day, when bread had been placed on the table for their meal, the pope asked Clare to bless it with the sign of the cross, but, feeling herself unworthy to pronounce a blessing in the presence of the Holy Father, she demurred. The pope then ordered her to bless the bread in the name of "holy obedience" to his wish, so that she would not perceive her blessing of the loaves to be presumptuous. The pope commanded

Clare to make the sign of the cross on the bread, and to bless it in God's name. Finally, in obedience to this command, Clare devoutly made the sign of the cross over the loaves of bread, each one of which immediately became clearly and miraculously marked with a cross!

Concurrently with the "Little Flowers" of Saint Francis and the charismatic preaching and egalitarian practices of the Cathars, including their efforts to make the Scriptures available in the vernacular, another gift for the Church apparently emerged from the fertile soil of southern Europe—a gift that has profoundly influenced the spiritual practice of the faithful. This was the Marian rosary. Popular tradition claims that the Virgin Mary herself revealed the rosary to Saint Dominic, the Spanish priest born in 1190 who established the Dominican order. Research, however, does not support this claim. The rosary seems to have evolved from the very ancient practice of the recital of the 150 psalms from the Hebrew Bible, called the Psalter. Monks, priests, and nuns recited these prayers in groups of fifty, while the laity substituted the "Our Father" and, later, a short form of the "Hail Mary" for the longer psalms they could not read. They counted their prayers on strings of beads or knots, a spiritual practice common to Moslems and Buddhists as well as some pagan cults from antiquity. The legend of Saint Dominic states that the Virgin appeared to him and requested that he say the "Angelic Psalter"—the greeting spoken by the angel Gabriel when he announced to Mary that she was chosen to be the mother of the Savior. Our Lady wished Dominic

to encourage the use of the prayer by the Roman Catholic faithful to combat the Albigensian heresy. The word rosary is derived from the old word *rosario* —meaning a "rose garden" or a "bouquet of roses"— and eventually this word replaced both the older terms, "Angelic" and "Marian Psalter."

Saint Clare, here depicted in the Church of San Francisco in Assisi, was a devoted follower of Francis.

Several centuries after its revival, thanks to the efforts of Dominic and his brother friars, the longer version of the "Ave Maria" was adopted, along with the three sets of "mysteries" concerned with important events in the life of Our Lady, as the basis for meditation during the time of prayer. The short mantra-like "Hail Mary" prayer often induces a deep meditative state, and the efficacy of the extended fifty-prayer sequence in achieving the intercession of the Virgin has been upheld universally. Devotees of Our Lady reflect on the mysteries as they finger their decades comprising ten beads and recite the memorized prayers which now include the "Our Father," at the beginning of each decade, the "Glory Be to the Father," and several other prayers, including the Apostles' Creed that begins the entire sequence.

Hail Mary, full of grace, the Lord is with thee.
Blessed art thou amongst women and blessed
is the fruit of thy womb. (ORIGINAL PRAYER OF
THE "ANGELIC PSALTER")

Holy Mary, Mother of God, pray for us
sinners, now and at the hour of our death.
Amen. (ADDITION TO THE MARIAN PRAYER)

MYSTERIES OF THE ROSARY

Five Joyful Mysteries:
The Annunciation
The Visitation
The Nativity
The Presentation of the Baby Jesus in the Temple
The Finding of the Child Jesus in the Temple

Five Sorrowful Mysteries:
The Agony in the Garden
The Scourging at the Pillar
The Crowning of Thorns
The Nailing of Jesus to the Cross
The Crucifixion and Death of Jesus

Five Glorious Mysteries:
The Resurrection of Jesus
The Ascension of Jesus into Heaven
The Descent of the Holy Spirit upon the Apostles
The Assumption of the Virgin Mary into Heaven
The Coronation of the Virgin Mary in Heaven

Five Luminous Mysteries:
The Baptism in the Jordan
The Wedding Feast of Cana
The Proclamation of the Kingdom of God
The Transfiguration
The Last Supper

PRACTICE: THE ROSARY

Ave Maria (Hail Mary)
Hail Mary, full of grace,
The Lord is with thee.
Blessed art thou amongst women
And blessed is the fruit of thy womb, Jesus.
Holy Mary, Mother of God,
Pray for us sinners,
now and at the hour of our death. Amen.

For those who are interested, a rosary can easily be made with beads or even with a long string knotted at equal intervals. The traditional rosary begins with an emblem, most often a crucifix, but another symbol might also be chosen, on which one lingers to say the Apostles' Creed. The next bead or knot represents the "Our Father" and is followed by three beads on which one says the "Hail Mary." The final bead in the introductory series is a second "Our Father." The other beads are arranged in decades, ten at a time, each bead representing one "Hail Mary." A single bead that represents an "Our Father" appears after each decade, and the five decades are all joined in a circle forming a band that bears a strong resemblance (intended or not!) to the astrological symbol for Venus. Each decade is an opportunity to meditate on one of the "Mysteries of the Rosary" and their order is prescribed as follows: the Joyful Mysteries are recited on Mondays, the Sorrowful Mysteries are recited on Tuesdays and Fridays, the Glorious Mysteries are recited on Wednesdays and Saturdays, and the newly proclaimed Luminous Mysteries are recited on Thursdays.

A shorter rosary called a "chaplet" is a popular alternative to the longer five-decade form. A chaplet usually has one decade of ten beads joined into a circle, again preceded by the five introductory prayers beginning with the crucifix. For a rosary honoring Mary Magdalene, the rosary loop should have seven groups of seven prayers each, while the chaplet's circle would have only seven beads or knots. Seven is the number sacred to the Holy Spirit and to "Wisdom": it unites the masculine "three" and feminine "four" from the cosmology of the ancient world. The rosary and chaplet will both have the same introductory sequence of five prayers. A variation of the traditional "Ave Maria" that might be said to honor the very popular "Beloved" of Jesus appears here:

Prayer to Mary Magdalene
Hail Mary, love incarnate,
The Lord is with you.
Chosen are you from all women,
and blessed is your union with Jesus.
Holy Mary, Beloved of Christ,
Pray for us now and in our hour of need. Amen.

CHAPTER SIX

MARIAN VISIONS

*And a great sign appeared in heaven: a woman was clothed
with the sun and the moon was under her feet, and on her head,
a crown of twelve stars.*

(REV. 12.1)

Marian Visions

Visions and visitations have inspired images like this well-known depiction of the "Sacred Heart of Jesus."

The appearance of a messenger from heaven is not a new phenomenon. In the ancient world, the goddess Isis apparently manifested herself to her devotees, and the Bible contains many similar experiences, including the angels who visited Abraham and Lot and the angel who accompanied Tobit on his journey in search of a bride. In the New Testament, Jesus appeared to his bereaved disciples after his Resurrection. During the two millennia of Christianity, visions have not been uncommon, and many, such as Saint Dominic's vision of "Our Lady of the Rosary," are a source of great spiritual consolation to the people. Often, an angel appears bearing a message from heaven, as when the archangel Gabriel visited Mary in Nazareth to inform her of her role as chosen mother of the Savior. In the case of the conversion of Paul, only the voice of Jesus was heard: a psychic phenomenon called a "locution"—inaudible words spoken directly to the heart and heard only in the mind. In the Gospel of John, Jesus appears to Mary Magdalene near the empty tomb on Easter morning and later breaks bread with two of his disciples in Emmaus. After that he appears to his disciples and allows Thomas to put his hands into the wounds on his hands and in his side. And he is seen again a few days later cooking fish on the shores of the lake where his disciples are out fishing. The Judeo-Christian Scriptures are full of physical manifestations of spiritual beings.

At the fifth-century Council of Ephesus, the Blessed Virgin Mary was officially named *Theotokos*, the "God-bearer," in response to the strong desire of the faithful who believed in her powerful intercession. She is the compassionate mediatrix of blessings and intercedes for supplicants at the throne of God. Under the aegis of the emperor Constantine, Christianity became a "solar" religion with a powerful hierarchy of male priests modeled on the Roman system of government, but the people insisted on balancing these elements with the irresistible archetype of feminine gentleness and love, the "Great Mother of God." When the delegates to the Council of Ephesus declared Mary the "God-bearer," the people of the city—formerly sacred to the Greek Goddess Artemis—were so overjoyed that they accompanied the assembled clergy in a torchlight procession back to their living accommodation at the close of the day's session. Devotion to the Virgin has been popular folk practice for centuries, filling the need to offset the high Christology and the Trinity of masculine energies found in Christian theology and doctrine.

Because of the relative frequency of Marian visions, recent theory suggests that visions of the Sacred Feminine are a psychic phenomenon projected from the communal need to connect with some archetypal aspect of itself that is not being sufficiently acknowledged. If it is the "Mother" or the "Feminine" that is taken for granted and not given its place of honor, that principle or archetype manifests itself in visions. This seems to be a rational explanation for an essentially irrational experience—one appearing to descend from heaven itself. The bulk of recorded visions were received by those in religious orders or ministry while alone at prayer or, in some famous instances, by simple children, of whom a number have been shepherds tending their flocks in the fields near their homes. The prototype for these visions is found in the Gospel of Luke, where the birth of the infant Savior was proclaimed to humble shepherds.

Joan of Arc

Across the wide green meadows of Champagne the bells of Domrémy were ringing, summoning villagers from the fields and the pious to evensong, but Joan could not hear them. Oblivious to her surroundings, she was listening to her "voices" with rapt attention. She had even for the moment forgotten her sheep. Saint Margaret and Saint Catherine were conversing with her, revealing the great mission she was to accomplish. Joan was to don a knight's armor and present herself to a local nobleman who would be persuaded to

accompany her to the dauphin of France. She would offer to lead his armies to victory against the English and Burgundians who were allied against the young weak heir to the French throne. Joan

Joan of Arc, the shepherdess "Maid of Orléans," led her nation's troops to victory and saw the dauphin crowned king in the Cathedral of Notre Dame at Rheims, where her statue now stands.

In 1858, Saint Bernadette Soubirous' visions of the Blessed Virgin brought about the cult of Our Lady of Lourdes. Saint Bernadette's image, like this statue in the Wienerwald, Germany, is universally revered.

later admitted to her accusers that she not only heard voices, but saw visions of various saints, although she was reluctant to speak of them in any great detail to the inquisitors who questioned her in prison.

Her voices did not mislead her. Possibly convinced by widely circulated prophecies about a "Maid of Orléans" who would lead them to miraculous victory, the soldiers of the French prince were inspired to follow Joan into battle. They defeated the foreign invaders and Joan was able to see the dauphin crowned king of France at the great cathedral of Notre Dame in Rheims, but soon the fortunes of the French army changed again, and Joan was betrayed and captured. The newly crowned king made no attempt to secure her freedom when she was subjected to trial and convicted of heresy by an ecclesiastic court. On May 30, 1431, at the pathetically young age of nineteen, and still believing in the authenticity of her visions, Joan of Arc was burned at the stake and her ashes thrown into the Seine.

Margaret-Mary Alacoque

Because she is considered more accessible and less judgmental than the Omnipotent Creator of the Cosmos, often it is Our Lady who appears to a faithful disciple, although some visionaries have also reported seeing Jesus himself. Perhaps the name of Margaret-Mary Alacoque's hometown in France—L'Hautecour—subconsciously influenced her to focus on the heart of the Beloved and his sufferings. Or perhaps it was her birth date—the feast day of Saint Mary Magdalene, July 22,

1647—that silently persuaded Margaret-Mary to focus on the wounded heart of the eternal Bridegroom. Even as a child, she was devout and cultivated the spiritual life, ignoring the pleasant activities and entertainments of youth and instead concentrating her energy on pious and ascetic practices, especially meditations on the sufferings of Jesus and on severe self-denial that ruined her health. At the age of seventeen she had a vision of Jesus scourged. He reproached her for infidelity, because she had not fulfilled her childhood promise to become a nun. Margaret-Mary entered the convent of the Visitation order where she was tested and unkindly ridiculed by some of the community for her claims to be a visionary.

After a vision of the "Sacred Heart" of Jesus surrounded by a crown of thorns and inflamed with love for humanity, she began her practice of hour-long midnight vigils lying prostrate before the Blessed Sacrament and receiving Holy Communion at Mass on the first Friday of every month. Margaret-Mary became the apostle of the First Friday devotion to the Sacred Heart of Jesus, a practice that spread throughout the Roman Catholic Church.

In parishes all around the world, women gather for Mass and First Friday devotions to the Sacred Heart of Jesus, while the Immaculate Heart of Mary is honored in similar liturgies on the first Saturday. The love of Christ and Mary for the faithful is unconditional. The great Basilica of Sacré Coeur on the holy hill above Montmartre, a site of pilgrimage since Druidic times, attests to the power of the "Sacred Heart."

Our Lady of Lourdes

Another youthful shepherdess, Bernadette Soubirous, was similarly chosen to receive visions from heaven. On February 11, 1858, the adolescent daughter of impoverished peasants in the Pyrenean village of Lourdes was startled by a loud noise coming from a cave in a hillside near her home. From a shimmering light hovering in the grotto a form emerged—that of a "Beautiful Lady." Over a period of about six months, Bernadette saw the Lady on eighteen separate occasions, people often gathering to watch when she went to the grotto to visit the Lady. One day the "Beautiful Lady" asked Bernadette to drink from the fountain in the grotto. Those present, who could not see the heavenly vision, but could only watch Bernadette's demeanor in her presence, were amazed to see the child digging energetically in the dirt wall of the grotto, where the earth suddenly gave way to a strong gush of water from an underground spring. Word of the miracle spread rapidly and people flocked to the site, bringing their ailments and injuries for healing in the waters of the holy spring.

. . . the most beautiful I have ever seen.
(BERNADETTE, DESCRIBING THE LADY OF HER VISION)

Through Bernadette, the Lady of the visions requested that a chapel be built on the hill near the grotto, and there the cult of Our Lady of Lourdes has grown steadily in popularity over the last century and a half. A huge basilica now adorns the hill, and processions of the sick and infirm stream steadily from the large plaza in front of the cathedral, down the slope on the right side and behind the church into the grotto area. Some supplicants are in wheelchairs, others on crutches. Friends and family members convey the paralyzed and critically ill on stretchers. Most pilgrims to Lourdes bring rosaries which they pray at the site, begging for favors from the merciful Queen of Heaven. Many bring empty vessels with them, which, after visiting the grotto and praying for the intercession of the "Beautiful Lady," they fill with fresh spring water from faucets lined up near the cave so that they can carry the sacred waters of Lourdes back to their homes and communities. Numerous unexplained and miraculous healings are attributed to Our Lady of Lourdes, and hers is one of the preeminent Marian shrines in the world, continuing to attract throngs of pilgrims of every faith from every nation on earth.

O clement, O loving, O sweet Virgin Mary. Pray for us, O holy Mother of God, that we may be made worthy of the promises of Christ.
(SHORT PRAYER TO OUR LADY)

Fatima

Another site famous for appearances of Mary in modern times is Fatima, a town in Portugal. This time, the Blessed Mother appeared to three young cousins who were tending their families' sheep on a hillside near their village. The eldest, Lucy de Jesus Santos, the youngest of seven children, was accompanied by her two younger cousins, Jacinta and Francisco Martos. The families were devoutly Catholic and the children said the rosary every day after lunch. On May 13, 1917, they had gone out to pasture their sheep as usual. Suddenly a bright light appeared above a small holm oak tree and they saw a vision of the "Beautiful Lady," who requested that they pray the rosary every day and return to the same site in a month's time.

Lucy had intended to keep the apparition secret, but Jacinta somehow blurted the whole story out to her mother. When the story spread, some villagers were angry and accused the children of lying. They were mocked and bullied by local priests and officials, but the little shepherds remained steadfast, returning each month to see the Lady as she had requested. The final visitation occurred near Fatima on October 13, 1917, and is now associated with the "miracle of the sun" reported at the scene. It had rained heavily the night before and the throngs of pilgrims—estimated at about seventy thousand—who streamed toward the site were soaked, muddy, and disheveled when they arrived, many on foot, at the site of the holm oak where the visions had previously occurred. They watched the children intently. Lucy, Francisco, and Jacinta were staring with rapt attention at the area above the oak. Our Lady asked them to have a chapel built at the site and told them that she was "Our Lady of the Rosary." As she prepared to leave, the sun suddenly broke through the dark storm clouds and began spinning. As the crowd stared, it spun violently in the heavens and then appeared to fall toward earth,

Jacinta Martos was the youngest out of the three cousins who saw visions of Our Lady at Fatima in 1917.

lasted about eight minutes, according to several witnesses. Many of the spectators had sunk to their knees in the mud, and were now amazed to see that their sodden coats and mud-clogged shoes were miraculously dry.

Our Lady entrusted the children at Fatima with a three-part secret, which Lucy revealed to Church prelates at intervals, the final portion to be revealed only after 1960. Little Jacinta and her brother Francisco both died of influenza within a year of the final apparition, but Lucy became a Carmelite nun, devoting her life to prayer and intercession for the Church. She wrote down the final part of the secret of Fatima and gave it to the pope for safekeeping. Pope John XXIII read the secret in 1959 and was allegedly so horrified by its implications that he decided not to make it public. Paul VI also decided to keep it secret, while John Paul II, believing that its most horrific aspects had already been fulfilled by the disintegration of the Communist Soviet Union and the thwarted attempt to murder him in 1981 on the feast of Our Lady of Fatima, allowed Lucy's final revelation to

coming closer and closer in a dizzying spiral. The crowd panicked, thinking that the sun would surely fall to the earth and explode, and an anguished moan erupted from the assembly, but before hitting the earth, the wildly whirling sun reversed itself and ascended back into its accustomed place in the sky. The entire event

Many artistic studies of the deposition of Christ often show the grieving Madonna weeping over the body of her Son.

be published in 2000. Its details described persecution and execution of members of the Church hierarchy by an army of soldiers. But the real eventualities of this act were believed to have been averted when the bullets of the would-be assassin, shot point-blank at the pope, were miraculously deflected.

Invariably, the message of Our Lady is one of conversion and repentance: Turn away, O sinners, from the path that leads to destruction. Amend your lives, return to God with prayer and contrition. Live at peace with one another. Shun immorality, vice, and violence; fast and pray. Attend Church services and remember to pray the rosary. Give up your selfish ways, your pleasure seeking, and your feuds. She sounds much like a mother voicing admonitions and instructions to her children, hoping they will heed her advice and take seriously her concern for their welfare. Patiently, she offers us the means to holiness. But many do not hear her pleas, do not heed her warnings. Is it any wonder that the statues of the "Beautiful Lady" are crying?

Tears of the Madonna

A recent phenomenon reported in the media in the past decade involves statues of the Virgin Mary in numerous churches around the globe that actually shed tears. Science is at a loss to explain these occurrences, which appeal enormously to the folk imagination. This occurrence of tears spontaneously flowing from the eyes of the Virgin Mary is not new. In 1681, an icon of the "Mother of God" was painted by a Romanian Orthodox priest and brought to the monastery of Nicula. Some Austrian officers stopped by at the monastery to make a visit to the church in 1694 and noticed that the icon of Our Lady was weeping. The icon continued to cry for nearly four weeks, and, as word of the miracle spread, people came to touch the tears of the Madonna and were miraculously healed of their ailments. When a Hungarian nobleman took the icon away, the Romanian peasants demanded its return, and a church was built on the hill near the village of Nicula to house the precious painting. It was moved several times in the twentieth century to keep it safe from the Communist authorities, but in March, 1992, escorted by a procession of pilgrims and devotees walking thirty miles, the *Theotokos* was returned to the monastery of Nicula, where she is honored by throngs of pilgrims who flock to her shrine, especially on the feast of the Assumption of Mary on August 15 of each year.

From remote village churches in the hills of Mexico, to Sidney, Australia, and Lake Ridge, Virginia, in the USA, stories have proliferated. Mary's statue is crying salt tears, often healing tears, occasionally tears of blood. In Barberton, Ohio, in 1992, a painting of Our Lady in Saint Jude's Orthodox Church amazed the parish by crying, and in 1996 in Lewis, Kansas, a six-inch high statue of Our Lady of Guadalupe manifested a similar phenomenon. In Civitavecchia, Italy, a statue brought from Medjugorje attracts thousands of pilgrims daily, often arriving in a line of chartered buses from all over Europe. In Trinidad, a replica of Our Lady of Lourdes manifested tears of blood, as did a statue belonging to Mary Murray, the postmistress in Grange Con, Ireland; another in Akita, Japan, was seen to cry numerous times over a period of six years, between 1975 and 1981. Silent but eloquent, the tears of the Madonna touch the hearts and often transform the lives of pilgrims who stream to these and other shrines of the Holy Mother across the globe.

Even the stones cry out, but the clergy still ask—why? Why does Our Lady cry? Any child knows the answer: the Holy Mother cries because she is sad. She stands in alcoves, on altars, in grottos, on pedestals, tears flowing from her eyes, and people ask why she is crying. She cries because she experiences the misery of her "little ones"—the poverty, suffering, and pain of the world, wars and famine, wounds and deprivation, and the consequences of sin, aptly defined as the "hardening of the human heart."

Our Lady does not limit her appearances to visions. She comes to us also in dreams. Often her face is dark. In our dreams she kneels at the bedside of an injured child and kisses a wounded knee. Or she stretches out her arms and embraces us with a warmth we have never known before. Sometimes she reaches out her hand holding a rosary, inviting us to pray. Sometimes she hands us a flower—a lily or a rose, traditional emblems of Our Lady. One woman reports a significant Marian dream: People gathered in the large church are expectant and the bishops, arrayed in their finest brocade vestments and wearing their high pointed hats, are assembled around the high altar. Everyone is awaiting the momentous event. Our Lady, the Queen of Heaven and Earth, is coming. She is expected at any moment. There is an excited buzz in the church, steadily increasing. And then suddenly, there is a deep hush. She has arrived! The ushers throw open the doors. A young woman with long dark hair and olive skin enters through the massive doorway of the church. She is barefoot, dressed in a long white linen gown of utmost simplicity that sways gracefully as she walks. Silently she walks down the aisle of the great cathedral built in her honor. She walks all the way to the steps in front of the main altar. She turns and faces the people for a few moments. The people are eager to hear what she will tell them. And then, just as silently as she came, she slowly walks back down the long aisle past the pews of amazed onlookers and back outside, where she gradually disappears into the distance. The people's awe is palpable.

Open your hearts to the Holy Spirit. Especially during these days the Holy Spirit is working through you.
(MESSAGE OF MARY AT MEDJUGORJE, MAY 23, 1985)

Medjugorje

In Yugoslavia, in June 1981, six young people from the village of Medjugorje (in present-day Bosnia-Herzegovina) began receiving visions and messages from Our Lady. Literally hundreds of messages have been conveyed, continuing to the present time. In spite of the gunfire and missiles dropping all around them, the village was not touched by the ethnic war in Bosnia. Pilgrims continue to flock to the site to honor the Lady, whose only message is "Pray!" She asks us to pray for peace and reconciliation, to pray by fasting, to pray with intensity, to pray now and always. She asks that we be open to the work of the Holy Spirit, that we be "vessels" as she was a vessel, allowing God's Word to become flesh in us.

Over the centuries, the message of Our Lady is unchanged. She has a litany of epithets: Queen of Peace, Mother of Sorrows, Queen of the Afflicted, Our Lady of the Roses. Universally, people of many faiths and creeds honor the manifestation of the Divine as "Great Mother"—in Christianity, her name is Mary.

In recent years, women have also received visions of Mary Magdalene in increasing numbers, and often of the Magdalene and Christ together. Joan Cameron Mitchell, an artist friend of one visionary, rendered one such vision in a drawing. Together the two women stood on a windy street corner and handed out copies of the picture to people attending a national conference. The tenderness of the "Christ couple" is poignantly conveyed in the drawing. It is called *Forgiveness* and portrays reconciliation at many levels.

Another woman reports a vision of Mary Magdalene, dressed in rough homespun gown, her dark tresses covered with a veil. She is walking slowly through a refugee camp, now pausing to greet a wretched bystander, now stooping to hug a waif and brush the tears from his eyes or to comfort an elderly invalid lying on a pallet on the ground. Her essence is compassion.

Still another woman shares a vision. She finds herself surrounded by women in biblical dress, gossiping and sharing their news as they fill their large water jugs at the village well. They are speaking a "Marian" language, she knows, but rather than the tongue of the Mother Mary, it is that of the Magdalene that she hears. She senses that she is to remain with these women, the "water carriers," and learn their language and wisdom.

Annette Hulefield from the American Midwest shares her dream experiences of Mary Magdalene. Here is her description of a dream that occurred on New Year's Day, 1998, the Feast of the Solemnity of Mary:

Mary the Mother of God appears in a vision and tells me quietly that she is leaving me. She has been my guide and healer for years, my Mother since forever. I begin to weep and beg her not to go. She says: "It is time for you to bring forth the other Mary." She fades into the distance and the Magdalene appears, beautifully garbed in red and orange silks, dancing joyously with a chalice. I cry and ask that this not be asked of me. I am ignorant and unworthy and confused.

Several years later, Annette had another significant dream:

I am standing on a riverbank, dressed as Magdalene, in a beautiful deep red cloak. I observe an idyllic, pastoral scene in which the Tree of Life is fully bloomed and the River of Life is flowing with ease. I can see its clarity and the many stones that are beautifully arranged under the surface. Suddenly, Jesus appears, dazzling as a star. He walks effortlessly; almost gliding in front of him is a swirling galaxy, perhaps the Milky Way. This energy never touches the ground, and with total awe, I watch as Jesus and the energy attune perfectly to each other, each dancing with unsurpassed grace and elegance. Jesus points to the center of the energy, indicating with his eyes that I am to come and step into the energy. In looking for a way to cross the river, I notice a newly constructed wooden bridge out of the corner of my eye. In an instant, I know it is an illusion and awaken, deeply anguished. Upon waking, I wondered why I had not used the path of the stones to cross the river.

In interpreting her ongoing experience of the Jesus/Magdalene paradigm of partnership, the prophetic dreamer explains that the shift from the traditionally accepted Lord/penitent disciple paradigm of Christ and Magdalene to the "partnership paradigm of the Beloveds" will not come through research and scholarship, but rather from the intuitive path of direct mystical communication of dreams and visions—the true "gnosis" of the seeker, poet, and visionary. It is through such dreams as these that the sacred union of the masculine and feminine energies/polarities will be manifested in the human psyche, the community, and the world.

PRACTICE: DREAMS

Dreams are messengers from our unconscious realm, and recording dreams is a time-honored tool for getting in touch with one's interior life. Dreams speak the language of the emotions and enlighten us about our most closely guarded feelings—hopes, fears, yearnings, and attitudes. For this spiritual practice, keeping a blank notebook and pen at your bedside is important, so that you can record a dream as soon as you awaken before the details dissolve into incoherent wisps. Some people tuck a notebook under their pillow to encourage dreams. It is helpful to make conscious your intent to record your dreams by actually stating the intent aloud as you get ready for bed. You might even like to invoke the Holy Spirit as your guide and mentor to help you get in touch with your dreams. At first, you may only remember scraps and shreds of a dream, but if you continue to record everything you remember on awakening, your ability to remember details will increase. Many books that address the content of dreams and symbols often found in dreams are available. The more consciously you pursue your dreams, the more likely you are to receive the full enlightenment and message that they bring, usually connecting you more intimately with your own emotions.

CHAPTER SEVEN

WALKING IN THE SPIRIT

For behold, I am with you always,
even until the end of the age.

(MATT. 28.20)

Walking in the Spirit

In the back corner of his monastery kitchen, the heavy man dressed in a monk's habit and smeared apron sat on a solid wooden stool paring vegetables and cutting them into a huge kettle. While his knife moved methodically, Brother Lawrence was oblivious to his steamy surroundings—the aroma of the soup simmering on the open hearth and the beads of sweat forming on his own brow. He was too intent on the conversation in which he was immersed to notice. Brother Lawrence was talking to God.

This stout seventeenth-century Carmelite brother was the humblest of monks, doing scullery and other menial tasks in the monastery of the Decalced Carmelites in Paris. Born in Lorraine to a family surnamed Herman, and baptized Nicholas, he had been wounded as a young man fighting in the Thirty Years War. Haunted and tormented by memories of the brutalities of war, he had sought refuge in the religious life where he developed a unique spirituality, so powerful and appealing that bishops sought his kitchen begging him to share his wisdom. Brother Lawrence sought union with God by a method he called "practicing the presence of God." God was not far away, out there somewhere

It is not necessary to be at Church to be with God. We can make a prayer room in our heart where we can return now and then to converse with him.
(BROTHER LAWRENCE, THE PRACTICE OF THE PRESENCE OF GOD, LETTER)

seated on a throne in a heaven above the clouds. God was near. God was present. God was always accessible. Only two things were needed, according to Brother Lawrence: complete abandon and trust in God's love and a constant, ongoing personal conversation with God on all matters, no matter how trivial. One did not need liturgies or memorized prayers, litanies, or sacraments. One need only speak with God spontaneously from the heart in constant communion and attentiveness. This ongoing conversation was not limited to times set aside for prayer, but was a continuous stream of consciousness directed to God at all times, in all places and circumstances. God was available even when one was, like this gentle monk, cleaning dishes or scrubbing vegetables. It's small wonder that women responded warmly to such homespun spiritual teachings as these! If one discovered that an interruption had occurred, one could immediately return to the conversation, picking it up anywhere and continuing the intimate communion—heart to heart with God.

Recorded conversations and letters containing teachings of Brother Lawrence were compiled and published in the late seventeenth century. Among them we find surprisingly candid statements: Brother Lawrence felt more united with God in his ordinary activities than when he devoted himself to religious activities, which left him with a profound spiritual dryness. The best way of reaching God, he declared, was to do ordinary daily tasks entirely for the love of God. His prayer was all day, every day, so that everything he did or said or thought was part of his prayer. The prayer of Brother Lawrence was his life, and his life became his prayer. He did not need a cathedral or a cardinal's hat—he was in constant union with God while paring potatoes or cleaning pots in his kitchen, confident that these simple acts were pleasing to God.

In a letter written to a priest who had requested spiritual counsel, Brother Lawrence related that he often imagined himself to be a block of stone presented to a sculptor, ready to be sculpted into a statue. He begged that God would form his perfect image in his soul. In a later missive addressed to a reverend mother, Brother Lawrence admits that he had at first sought God by reading several spiritual books, but discovered that they were a hindrance to him in his quest to belong wholly to God. Among the benefits of the practice of God's presence is its profound effect of making faith more alive and active in all circumstances, especially during times of need. It also increases hope in God's goodness and generosity and reliance on his mercy.

For those suffering from the fragmentation of modern life, this practice of union with God is a sure sanctuary. The erudite and lofty writings of Church fathers like Augustine and Aquinas have not fed the spirituality of the Christian laity as have the spiritual teachings of the humble brother scrubbing floors and dishes wholly for love of God. His teachings spread among Christians in the form of a tiny book, *The Practice of the Presence of God*, and became widely popular, influencing generations that followed to achieve conscious union with God as a spiritual practice. The homely sincerity and simplicity of this "way" had enormous appeal, especially for the poor, the uneducated, and women—those who were often confined to harsh lives of menial labor. According to Brother Lawrence, such lives were not a hindrance to spirituality, but its means!

We have an infinitely gracious God who knows our every need.
(BROTHER LAWRENCE, *THE PRACTICE OF THE PRESENCE OF GOD*, LETTER)

Out of Egypt

This homely understanding of a God who cares deeply about the well-being of each individual is rooted in the Gospels. We are not to be anxious about tomorrow or about the food we eat or the clothes we wear: "Consider the lilies of the field; they neither toil nor spin"—but they are more richly arrayed than Solomon in all his glory. How much more does God care for his people! Assurances of God's all-encompassing love have nurtured Christians through the most desperate struggles and hopeless situations. One powerful example is found in the plight of the Africans captured by traders and brought to the shores of America to be sold into slavery, forced to do hard physical labor on the large plantations in the southern states, reaping tobacco and picking cotton. The black slaves brought with them a love of music and sense of rhythm that found its unique expression in the "Negro spirituals," a genre of music beloved around the world for its depth of

furnace. They heard about Moses who led his people out of Egypt across the dry bed of the Red Sea miraculously formed by the power and benevolence of God. They also heard the Gospel stories of Jesus' healing ministry and his death on Calvary. The African slaves took these ancient stories, along with songs and psalms from the Scriptures, and

TRADITIONAL NEGRO SPIRITUALS

Let us break bread together on our knees.
Let us break bread together on our knees.
When I fall down on my knees with my face
to the rising sun,
Oh, Lord, have mercy on me.

"NOBODY KNOWS THE TROUBLE I SEE"
Nobody knows the trouble I see.
Nobody knows but Jesus.
Nobody knows the trouble I see.
Glory, Hallelujah!
Sometimes I'm up; sometimes I'm down
Oh, yes, Lord.
Sometimes I'm almost to the ground
Oh, yes, Lord.

"GO DOWN, MOSES"
When Israel was in Egypt Land
Let my people go!
Oppressed so hard he could not stand
Let my people go!
Go down, Moses. Way down in Egypt Land.
Tell old Pharaoh: "Let my people go!"

A gospel choir. Clapping, dancing, and stomping still accompany Gospel music in contemporary services, which are full of energy, spontaneity, and inspiration.

feeling and marvelous harmony and melody. As new converts to Christianity, slaves gathered to listen to itinerant preachers who told them favorite stories from the Hebrew Bible—the stories of the patriarchs Abraham and Jacob and of Joseph, sold like them into slavery; the story of Daniel in the lion's den and the Hebrew children in the fiery they turned them into their own spiritual chants, deeply evocative and powerful "corn ditties," as they were called. Stomping, clapping, and dancing often accompanied the performance of this new genre of Gospel music, which became a huge source of inspiration and encouragement to the oppressed slaves. They gathered at night after their worship services in their "praise houses" or at secret "camp meeting" sites in the woods or fields to sing their songs, drawing comfort from the camaraderie of their shared experience of suffering and their hope of salvation. The bonds forged during these nocturnal songfests around a bonfire and the comforting promises of Jesus nurtured a strong sense of community that gave the slaves emotional support to bear their miseries. Numerous abolitionists looking to their Christian principles of equality, freedom, and justice, sympathized with the plight of the slaves and in 1865 slavery was abolished in the United States.

Harriet Tubman

One of the most remarkable women of faith in American history is Harriet Tubman, born a slave in Maryland in 1820, the eleventh child of her parents. She worked as a nursemaid for years, and in 1849, fearing that she was going to be sold to a different owner, she decided to escape with two of her brothers. Some of the Negro spirituals contained coded instructions to "follow the drinking gourd" (the Big Dipper) to reach the "Promised Land" in the North, across the "Jordan"—the slaves' name for the Ohio River—to reach Philadelphia and safety. Harriet managed to escape this way, and in Philadelphia she befriended abolitionists. Over the next ten years, she was instrumental in leading other slaves to safety on the famous "Underground Railroad," ultimately helping more than three hundred of her people to "cross over." Over and over Harriet returned to the South risking capture at every turn, in order to help others escape the horrors and oppression of slavery. She was known as the "Moses of Her People," a messianic savior who defied those who placed a $40,000 reward on her head. During the Civil War she served as a nurse and was able to save numerous more lives with her knowledge of "old wives'" medicinal lore, including an effective remedy for dysentery, a disease which at the time was often fatal. The story of Harriet Tubman's selfless dedication in service to her people is reflected in the epitaph on her grave: "Servant of God. Well done."

Harriet Tubman escaped from slavery and led others out of oppression and into freedom.

Because of its emotional impact, music has always been part of the worship experience of the Christian community. The genre of Gospel music, a modern descendant of Negro spirituals, is sung by numerous popular artists in our day and is only the latest art form to grow out of the passionate yearning for intimacy with the Holy One.

Corrie ten Boom's house in Haarlem, in the Netherlands, was a secret refuge for Jews in the 1940s.

The desert communities of the earliest centuries sang and chanted psalms, and the Gregorian chants of medieval monasteries are available on CDs and often used for meditation. Sublime Requiem Masses and Oratoria were created from a deep reservoir of religious fervor and desire to praise the Creator. One does not have to be Christian to appreciate the ecstatic climax of the human spirit attained in Handel's *Messiah*, performed all over the globe year after year to huge and enthusiastic audiences. Christians treasure the liturgical music, hymns of praise and thanksgiving, and modern folk songs celebrating the Christian experience and the promises of Christ. Churches and schools have formed choirs to enhance their worship experience by sharing the rich tradition of Church music, for "he who sings, prays twice." Gospel singers like Anne Murray, Christy Lane, and Amy Grant have promoted the popularity of the genre around the entire globe, a powerful support to the international work of missionaries, for music is a universal language and the powerful message of Jesus Christ continues to transform lives.

Corrie ten Boom

An enduring characteristic common to committed Christians is an unshakable belief that the exhortations of Jesus must be literally obeyed. Also appealing is their simple and perfect trust that his promises will be fulfilled. The "Word of God" is their truth and their light. Many Christians have appeared almost childlike in their absolute faith and their literal acceptance of the words of Christ, living proof of his admonition that unless a person becomes as a little child, he will not enter the kingdom of heaven. Throughout the centuries, dedicated followers of the Gospel teachings of Jesus have been heroic in their steadfast faith, often in the face of dire circumstances. They take literally the Gospel Beatitude: "Blessed are those who suffer persecution for the sake of righteousness, for theirs is the kingdom of heaven" (Matt. 5.10). Thousands of lives could be found to illustrate this perfect faith, and beyond those, many more whose names and heroic feats are known only to God.

As witness to uncompromising faith in the words and promises of Christ, the names of two middle-aged Dutch spinsters come to mind—Elizabeth and Cornelia ten Boom. Their father, Casper ten Boom, was a clockmaker in Haarlem who owned a clock and watch repair shop. The ten Boom family, consisting of Casper, his invalid wife, two unmarried daughters, and their spinster aunts, lived above their shop in a house that had been the family residence for more than a hundred years. The lives of this family were typically middle class, deeply rooted in the community and church of their hometown. Casper was a devout Christian who read the Scriptures, both Hebrew and New Testament Bible passages, aloud to his family every morning and evening. His only son, Willem, became a minister of the Dutch Reformed Church and later ran a home for the elderly in a rural area not far from Haarlem.

Outwardly, this family seemed entirely ordinary and lived very quiet, normal lives until that disastrous night in May, 1940, when the Netherlands surrendered to Hitler's invading army and the panzers and trucks of the Third Reich rolled through the streets of Haarlem bearing German soldiers. For a while, the situation remained fairly normal under the German occupying forces, but when Jewish clients of their shop began to disappear under unexplained circumstances, the ten Booms sensed that something was terribly wrong. Gradually they began reaching out to people in need, and over a period of months, their house became a headquarters for the Resistance, helping downed Allied pilots and Jews escape from the occupied Netherlands. A false wall was built in Corrie's upstairs bedroom, creating an extra, secret room behind what looked like an old built-in bookcase. Here a constant flow of Jewish refugees found safe haven until they could be smuggled safely out of Haarlem and to the coast where they could be picked up by boat and ferried across the channel to safety in the British Isles. The Dutch Resistance network was dedicated and effective.

In spite of the obvious danger of being caught and executed, Corrie, Betsie, and their father became ever more deeply committed to saving Jews, often harboring six or seven at a time, until the inevitable day of their betrayal. Unexpectedly, a German cohort raided their home and found enough evidence to indict them, although the six Jews currently residing in their household were safely sequestered in the secret room upstairs, from which they eventually managed to escape. The patriarch Casper, eighty-four years old, died in prison ten days later, but Corrie and Betsie were interned in several prisons in the Netherlands and then shipped to Ravensbruck in Germany. The conditions were deplorable, and the deprivation and squalor became worse as the war dragged on, but the two women managed to be staunch and inspired witnesses for Christ to the other women with whom they were incarcerated. Their family managed to smuggle them a small Dutch Bible that Corrie wore on a cord around her neck, like the persecuted Cathars of the thirteenth century. She and Betsie managed to preach and pray with the other women prisoners, and were amazed at the way their faith was upheld. On arrival at Ravensbruck in 1944, they were appalled at the miserable condition of the dormitory, which contained rows of stacked wooden pallets meagerly covered with flea-infested straw. Betsie, the frail older sister, thanked and praised God for the situation, including the fleas, while Corrie herself remained skeptical. Could God really be present in such conditions? She struggled to believe that God would not abandon them.

Mother Teresa with a child. She dedicated her whole life to bringing the love of Christ into the the unhappy and impoverished lives of the "untouchables" of Calcutta.

they discovered that the main reason the wardens avoided the dormitory was—the fleas! The fleas were, in fact, part of God's salvation plan for the women at the Ravensbruck concentration camp, providing safe cover for their forbidden ministry and Scripture study.

Corrie had managed to retain with her a small bottle of vitamin drops that she issued nightly to her emaciated sister. Other women, too, were in need of the vitamins, so Corrie gave them drops as well. She kept wondering when the vitamins in the little dark brown bottle would finally run dry, but each night there was still a trickle of golden brown liquid in the dropper to be dispensed to women in the dormitory, like the oil in the menorah of the Maccabees that never ran dry, the story at the heart of the Jewish Hanukkah celebration. Miracles like this touched their hearts and kept their hope alive. Yes, God was true to his promises; he was with them always. Even in a concentration camp in the heart of Germany, in the silent snows and darkest nights of winter, in the raging theater of a world war, God was there.

Betsie died in the camp at Ravensbruck, but Corrie survived to return to Holland, where she dedicated the rest of her life to rehabilitating lives broken and ruined by the war, eventually even returning to Germany to help the countrymen of those who had held her prisoner. Her autobiography, *The Hiding Place*, is an inspiration to readers of all ages. Here was a woman who had no intention of being a heroine; the joy of the Lord was her strength and the strength of the Lord whom she served upheld her incredible faith.

The two sisters were surprised to find that the surly women wardens at Ravensbruck rarely ventured into the dormitory, which left the two sisters free to pray and minister to the women there relatively undisturbed. Toward the end of the war,

Mother Teresa

On the other side of the world, in the middle of the twentieth century, another woman was answering a spiritual calling she had received to serve the poor and dying on the streets of Calcutta. Gnarled and emaciated hands of impoverished homeless and "untouchables" reached imploringly toward this tiny woman in her coarse white and blue sari. Mother Teresa and her religious sisters, known as the Sisters of Charity, made the squalid streets of this teeming metropolis their home. Born in 1910, to middle-class parents in Yugoslavia, Agnes Gonxha Bojaxhiu lost her father when she was only nine years old. Her mother managed to raise her three children and to educate them. When she was eighteen, Agnes felt the call to be a missionary sister in India. She joined the Sisters of Loreto, taking the name Sister Teresa, and received training in the religious life; then she journeyed to India, where she took her vows in 1931 and trained to become a teacher. But her strongest call was to alleviate the misery of the poor. She finally received permission from her superiors to leave the Sisters of Loreto and receive medical training so that she could fulfill her vocation to serve the most impoverished of the poor. She wanted not only to help them; she wished to live with them, sharing their rice and salt. She wandered through the streets binding up wounds, washing babies, and feeding and comforting the sick, offering advice on nutrition and hygiene.

First one and gradually other young Bengali women were inspired by Sister Teresa's selfless devotion to the dregs of humanity and wanted to join her. They formed a community, called the Sisters of Charity. Garbed in cheap white and blue saris and sandals, with absolute selfless and wholehearted devotion they ministered to the malnourished and the destitute, the starving, and the terminally ill. Now known as Mother Teresa, their founder traveled all over the world soliciting financial support for her congregation of sisters and their charitable ministry. She was a legend in her own time, and already the Roman Catholic Church is preparing to canonize this tiny woman with a gigantic heart and monumental faith in Jesus and his message of love for the poor.

For I was hungry and you gave me food, I was thirsty and you gave me drink, a stranger and you welcomed me . . . whatever you did to the least of my brothers you did unto me.
(MATT. 25.35, 40)

Missionaries in Afghanistan

In early fall 2001, a story broke on the television news channels in the United States. On August 3, Afghan officials had arrested and imprisoned two American women accused of preaching the Gospel and trying to convert Muslims to Christianity in a remote town in the mountains somewhere in northern Afghanistan. Their families were frantic. Several family members were interviewed on television fervently asking for prayers for their daughters, who worked for a German relief agency called "Shelter Now," providing shelters for the homeless. The two women, Dayna Curry from Tennessee and Heather Mercer from

Heather Mercer, who was arrested by the Taliban in 2001, worked for a relief agency in rural Afghanistan.

a new pair of tennis shoes to someone who was needy. Evidently, the call to help the poor was powerful for both women, who were willing to leave the comforts of home and travel around the world to live their Christian faith.

And now, they were confined with the other female aid workers in a cell in Kabul, with wars and the rumors of wars raging all around them—young, vulnerable, and in the hands of the repressive and misogynist Taliban regime. Urgent messages to pray for Heather and Dayna and their fellow prisoners went out to Christian churches all over the nation. Prayer vigils were arranged and petitions circulated. Everyone feared that these relief workers might be caught up in the violence threatening Afghanistan, or perhaps worse, that they would be convicted by the Taliban court of justice and executed for sharing their faith with Muslim women in their remote village.

Virginia, were incarcerated along with six other international workers—Peter Bunch and Diana Thomas from Australia, Georg Taubmann, Katrin Jelinek, Margrit Stebner, and Silke Durkopf from Germany—and sixteen native Afghans who were not identified by name. Both Americans had been students at Baylor University and had met while attending the Antioch Community Church, a non-denominational Christian evangelical church in Waco, Texas. Before moving to Afghanistan, Dayna Curry had worked with troubled youth in Waco, while Heather Mercer had just completed her undergraduate degree at Baylor, where she was involved in Baptist student ministries. One of her friends related a story about her having given away

A wave of relief swept across America on November 15 with the news that the American women had been released, along with their fellow workers. Their later news conference provided some details of their imprisonment. Dayna related that she had never felt closer to Christ than she did in prison, because her trust in him was all she had. She said that it was hard not knowing how it would all turn out, but she continued to have faith, knowing that the entire world was praying for them. Their jailors had been kind to them, the girls reported. The men had actually shared their own food with the prisoners. With an imminent attack expected on Kabul, the group was to have been moved to Kandahar, but the plans were disrupted and the prisoners were rescued. The ordeal of the previous few months, the uncertainty and deprivation, the fear of execution by hanging—the Taliban punishment for their offense—all had been borne in a courageous spirit of faith and trust in the Lord who was their Shepherd, Bridegroom, and King: "Though I walk through the shadow of death, I shall not fear." The two relief workers shared their faith that even in the far dungeons of Afghanistan, Christ was present, just as he had promised, to those who trust in him.

Contemporary Activists

At a recent convention, an international group of reform-oriented Roman Catholics, Dr. Elisabeth Schüssler Fiorenza gave an important keynote lecture focused on her vision for a church of women. During about five minutes of her talk, the renowned feminist theologian and professor from Harvard Divinity School spoke enthusiastically about this new church of women. She mentioned the phrase five or six times. Some of the women present began to be uncomfortable at the repeated use of the unaccustomed phrase. Finally a low mumble could be heard. The distinguished speaker cocked her ear, sensing that her audience did not like the sound of the phrase they thought sounded a bit exclusive. Smiling, she asked if they thought a church of women would not welcome men or permit them to hold important leadership positions. Perhaps they thought men might feel uncomfortable in a church of women. Then she explained that it would be very inclusive of men, just as the word "women" includes "men," as "she" includes "he," and "female" includes "male." She asserted there would be no discrimination against men in a church of women. Men would be welcome to participate!

The audience was laughing by the time she finished, but everyone present at the lecture got the point. The new church would certainly be a novelty on planet Earth: a New Song, indeed! But Dr. Schüssler Fiorenza does not actually recommend the church of women she described. She believes that the Christian community of the future must be one based on full gender equality and partnership modeled on the paradigm provided by the first generation of Christians —the men and women who walked with Jesus.

During the twentieth century, serious challenges were raised to the traditional exclusion of women from some Christian pulpits. The struggle for women's ordination was soundly based on the model provided in the New Testament texts that attest to the prominent roles of women in the first generation of the Church. Under steady pressure from women in their congregations, many Christian denominations have gradually loosened their strictures against women clergy and now many permit—even encourage—them to attend seminaries and divinity schools. Many in the worldwide Anglican communion were delighted

We need socially just Christian communities now. For the sake of the people, for the sake of the poor, for the sake of the Gospel, for the sake of the planet.[17]
(SISTER JOAN CHITTISTER[17])

when Barbara C. Harris was consecrated a bishop in the Episcopal Church in 1989 following a difficult period of controversy over her election to the office of "suffragan" (assistant) bishop. Several other women priests have since joined her in the hierarchy of the Anglican communion, and the dialogue is ongoing in many denominations. Only the Roman Catholic hierarchy has been unwilling to even address the possibility of ordaining women. Many Roman Catholic nuns are understandably unhappy with this rigid stance of the Vatican, especially when many Catholic parishes around the world are faced with serious shortages of ordained priests—shortages so severe that they threaten to create a crisis in the next generation.

Following the lead of feminist theologians like Mary Daly, sisters in numerous religious orders actively seek to change the official decision regarding the ban on women priests. These nuns serve as chaplains and religious education directors. Some are CEOs of large hospitals and deans of universities, but because of Church tradition they cannot say Mass. Among the most outspoken advocates of gender equality and ordination of women is an American Benedictine nun, Sister Joan Chittister, formerly a prioress of her community. Sister Joan is a strong and relentless advocate of human rights and gender equality, as well as environmental protection and social justice—a spiritual warrior in the tradition of the saint whose name she bears.

In addition to being the author of many books on contemporary spirituality, Sister Joan is often invited to give lectures at important gatherings and had expressed her desire to address those gathered at a conference attended by a group called "Women's Ordination Worldwide" in Dublin in the summer of 2001. The Vatican actually tried to prevent Sister Joan's participation at the conferences by requesting that her prioress, Sister Christine Valdmiroff, prohibit her from attending. After prayer and soul-searching, Sister Christine declined to cooperate with the Vatican's attempt to silence Sister Joan, declaring that she did not think that Sister Joan's participation at the conference in Dublin would cause scandal to the faithful, and further, that the faithful would only be scandalized when honest attempts to discuss important questions were forbidden!

Heresy is what the Church does not teach. Prophecy is what the Church doesn't teach yet! The voice of Sister Joan is like the voice of John the Baptist crying in the wilderness: "Prepare ye the way of the Lord." Along with other courageous women who have taken their discipleship seriously, she will not be silenced.

When asked, many Roman Catholics state that they would be glad to see women ordained, and an even greater number are willing to see married priests reinstated to serve in their parishes. Lifting the demand for priestly celibacy has strong advocates, especially in the past ten or fifteen years, as shortages of priests have become ever more noticeable. There are thousands of married priests quietly serving their communities who would be very willing to reassume official clerical roles if they were permitted.

Post-Roman Christianity

In the closing decade of the twentieth century, various movements surfaced that can be characterized as post-Christian in its narrowest sense. These movements seem to have grown out of the Charismatic movement and are characterized by an emphasis on relationship—that which unites rather than what separates. Such communities are inclusive, ecumenical, and centered on the action of the Holy Spirit. They seem to be an incarnation of Paul's sublime words from his First Epistle to the Corinthians: "If I speak with the tongues of men and of angels, and have not love, it profits me nothing!" These vibrant, Spirit-filled communities, based on the heart of the Gospel message, thrive in many places around the world, often meeting in people's homes rather than in churches. Perhaps one of the models for this phenomenon of home churches can be found in the stories about the brave citizens in Communist countries who risked their lives meeting for worship services between 1945 and 1989 when Christianity was severely suppressed. Missionaries smuggled Bibles into these lands, and the devout met stealthily behind closed doors to share their faith. Christianity in its purest and simplest form, radical faith in the love and mercy of God, seems to flourish under duress.

At the same time, a similar phenomenon was spreading in the democratic countries where freedom of religion is taken for granted. People began meeting in homes for prayer meetings and group Bible studies, often led by lay people. Spurred by the evangelical denominations, Christians from "liturgical" Churches joined in the

Sister Irma Dulce, known as the Mother Teresa of Brazil, embraces one of the children living in the orphanage she founded in Bahia.

movement. Charismatic prayer services featuring *glossolalia*, the ecstatic sounds and utterances known as "speaking in tongues," and spontaneous healings had long been a mainstay of Pentecostal denominations; but in the 1960s and 1970s, a new Pentecost leaped as if by spontaneous combustion across boundaries into virtually every Christian church. Catholics who had spoken Latin prayers by rote only a few years before began speaking in

tongues along with their Anglican, Lutheran, and Methodist friends. Prayer requests began circulating by telephone, and women met in thousands of small groups to pray for their families and communities. Often they took turns babysitting for the little ones while the young mothers met to study Scripture, sing hymns, and pray for miraculous healings for friends who were ill or injured. Pope John XXIII had organized the Second Vatican Council and had prayed for a "New Pentecost" to sweep through the Church, but no one envisioned the worldwide spread of "chapel homes" and small faith communities, rather like those of the earliest Christians.

Compassion for the poor and afflicted motivates this relief worker who is feeding a needy family in a shelter in Somalia. This is the essence of Christianity in action.

For there is neither Jew nor Greek, slave nor freeman, there is neither male nor female. For you are all One in Christ Jesus.

(GAL. 3.28)

He who drinks of the water that I shall give him will never thirst.

(JOHN 4.13)

One of the characteristics of the movement toward autonomous community gatherings was their ecumenism. No one asks to see baptismal certificates at home church gatherings. The Bible Study Fellowship International (BSF) is an example of a worldwide group that organizes Bible studies in home or church settings where anyone is welcome. Women meet in the daytime, couples and working singles at night. Even preschoolers are included in their programs, which meet weekly and follow a specific curriculum for an entire year. On military bases around the globe, nondenominational prayer services are offered; and Scripture classes are ongoing under the aegis of the Protestant Women of the Chapel (PWOC), which are often attended by Roman Catholics as well as other Christian women. The thirst for the "Word of God" is quenched in the "living water" that Jesus promises to those who ask.

One of the most unique Charismatic communities in the world is the ecumenical center founded by Brother Roger at Taizé in France. All through the year people from every continent gather at Taizé to meditate, to chant, and to pray in the Spirit. They come as pilgrims and stay for a day or several days, sometimes longer, basking in the peaceful and gentle light of the prayer community, conversing with the monks and other pilgrims and responding to the bells that call them three times a day to the prayer services in the Church of Reconciliation. The community welcomes people of all faiths and denominations, who flock by the thousands to the retreat center established by Brother Roger.

Another movement gathering momentum at the dawn of the third Christian millennium is the attempt to reclaim the "Aramaic Jesus." The idea seems to be a logical consequence of twentieth-century scholarship that worked to restore the "historical Jesus"—how he lived and died, what he said, what he meant—as opposed to the Jesus Christ of the Creed who rules from a throne "at the right hand of the Father" in heaven and judges "the living and the dead." The theory is that Jesus, being a native of first-century Palestine, probably spoke Aramaic rather than Greek. Many Scripture scholars believe he spoke both languages, since *koiné* Greek was the most common language throughout the eastern regions of the Roman Empire. It is believed that the Gospels were originally written in Greek, but if they were written from stories that circulated first in Aramaic, then the original flavor of the sayings of Jesus was sadly distorted in translation. Aramaic is a language very rich in associations, not nearly so rigid as Greek. Because there are fewer words, each one conveys several meanings at the same time. The translation work of Neil Douglas-Klotz in this field is seminal, providing us with a revolutionary new perspective on several

O Birther!
Father-Mother
of the Cosmos,
you create all that
moves in light.
(Translation: Our
Father which art
in heaven.)
(NEIL DOUGLAS-KLOTZ[18])

Free us to walk
your path with joy.
(Translation: Deliver
us from evil.)
(NEIL DOUGLAS-KLOTZ[19])

favorite passages from the Gospels—the "Our Father" and the Beatitudes found in the Gospel of Matthew, for example. These teachings of Jesus are rooted in the mystical desert tradition of his people, and his words in Aramaic would have had multiple layers of meaning—literal, metaphoric, poetic, mystical. The phrases of Aramaic are more inclusive, more holistic, more universal than their Greek translation. *Heaven* means more than "sky" or a "home in the sky" in Aramaic; it has connotations of "light" and "sound" reverberating throughout the entire universe, and the "kingdom of heaven" is always "among" and simultaneously "within" us.

In reclaiming the Aramaic prayers of Jesus, Douglas-Klotz emphasizes the need to experience the actual sounds of the Aramaic words as well as their multifaceted meanings. For each line of the "Our Father," Douglas-Klotz provides seven or eight alternative translations that help us to understand the phrase on different levels and from various points of view. Communities of Christians are now incorporating these translated Aramaic prayers into their worship services, experiencing deep healing and solace in the beautifully egalitarian and inclusive phrases of the earliest Christian prayers. They say aloud the Aramaic words, and then pray the translation. Along with these prayers, they are encouraged to incorporate body movements—they dance the Scriptures! This holistic incorporation of the physical with the mystical is a "sacred union" of the left and right brain spheres and is deeply moving and enlightening for the communities that embrace it.

The modern trend away from legalism, rigidity, and doctrine continues, resulting from the recent resurgence of interest in the Sacred Feminine in her various aspects: the Virgin, the Goddess, and the Holy Spirit. Post-Roman Christians take pilgrimages to sacred sites around the world, including shrines of the Black Madonna and those of Marian apparitions, in record numbers. Responding to the call of the Mother, they reach out to the marginalized and the disenfranchised. Soup kitchens for the homeless, shelters for abused spouses, food drives at all seasons of the year, and gratuitous acts of charity are sometimes linked to a specific church or faith community, but many are ecumenical and occur outside the walls of institutional religion. It seems that the people themselves are taking responsibility for being the "vessels" of compassion, of positive action, and of change. In some small faith communities, women are actually leading the liturgies as of old. Sheila D. Dierks is a pioneer who encourages women to lift their voices and claim their priestly role by celebrating liturgies. She owns WovenWord Press, a small publishing firm dedicated to publishing spiritual works written by women, and has recently published several books of inclusive liturgies including a surprisingly refreshing collection of such prayers called *New Wine*, which were written by Mary T. Beben.

In 1991, a lay Catholic in Farmington, Massachusetts, was desperately looking for a priest to come to to visit her mother who was seriously ill in a nursing home. She contacted her parish priest, only to be told he was too busy and, in calling around frantically to nearby parishes, Louise Haggett was unable to find any priest willing to visit her mother, who had been a devout Roman Catholic all her life. This painful experience led Louise to found an organization she named "Celibacy is the Issue" or "CITI," which in less than ten years has grown in numbers and enthusiasm and is now an international network of priests who have left the clerical state or been "laicized." The organization is supportive of married Roman Catholic priests who wish to return to active ministry, encouraging them to become a priestly presence in their communities by offering to perform weddings and baptisms and other sacraments of the Church. Their services are fully accepted by civil authorities. Many of these priests work in partnership with their wives, some of whom were nuns themselves. They give counsel and spiritual direction to those who request it. Some are chaplains in hospitals or universities, some work as counselors and therapists. They minister to the lonely, the marginalized, the ostracized, and divorced Catholics. Their work includes men and women who are gay and lesbian. Married priests allow their conscience to be their guide, while asking themselves: "What would Jesus do?"

Priestly celibacy as practiced in the Roman Catholic Church is a relatively late demand imposed in the mid-twelfth century, ostensibly to prevent priests' offspring from laying claim by inheritance to Church property. This demand for priestly celibacy is not rooted in the Christian Scriptures; according to Saint Paul's First Epistle to the Corinthians, the brothers of Jesus and the other apostles traveled with their "sister-wives" on their missionary journeys. Yet this model of missionary partnership has been denied for eight hundred years in the largest Christian denomination. The Protestant reformers of the sixteenth century wisely renounced the vow of celibacy on the grounds that it was neither advisable nor scriptural, citing the fact that the apostles were married and also the Book of Genesis to justify their stance: "It is not good for the man to be alone. I will make a partner for him" (Gen. 2.18). Martin Luther, the great Protestant reformer who attacked the corrupt practice of selling indulgences, and also other abuses by the Church, was a former Roman Catholic priest. After taking his stand against the Catholic Church, he married a former nun named Katherina von Bora, with whom he had a family of six children.

Do we not have the right to take along with us a sister-wife as do the other apostles and the brothers of the Lord and Cephus.
(SAINT PAUL'S EPISTLE, 1 COR.9.5)

For its model for repudiating women as priests, the Roman Catholic hierarchy cites, not the apostles, but Christ himself. This example is, however, controversial, especially in light of strong evidence that marriage was customary for a rabbi in first-century Judaism. Since Jesus was Jewish, he was most probably married,[20] and further evidence suggests that his loving relationship with his "sister-bride" probably formed the model for sacred union at the heart of the infant Christian community in Jerusalem. While it is certain that the model for the missionary couples spreading the "Good News" in the first generation of Christianity was not Paul, it seems more likely that the model may well have been Jesus.

Was sacred union the cornerstone that the builders rejected when erecting the edifice of Christian doctrine? Perhaps this was the original meaning of the parable Jesus told about the king who held a marriage feast for his son. In the story, the invited guests found excuses for not attending the wedding banquet, so the servants were sent out to round up strangers from off the highway, and even many of these were reluctant to come to celebrate the feast: "For many are called, but few are chosen" (Matt. 22.14). Perhaps it was precisely this—Christ's radical embrace of the Feminine/Sophia with all her sacred attributes of compassion, wisdom, inclusiveness, tenderness, tolerance, and love—that many of his contemporaries were unable to accept. The banquet was prepared, the table set for the sacred union at the heart of the kingdom of God, but most refused to celebrate the true partnership and psychic wholeness inherent in gender equality.

Among the Gnostic Christians of the first three centuries of the Christian era, it was Mary Magdalene who was honored as the incarnation of the "Sophia." This view is confirmed by the gematria encoded in the New Testament Gospels.

The consort of the Savior is Mary . . . and Christ loved her more than all the disciples and used to kiss her often on her mouth.
(NAG HAMMADI LIBRARY, GOSPEL OF PHILIP[21])

The system of using numerical values of words to enhance their meaning identifies the Magdalene with the ratio associated with the (), the *Vesica Piscis*, the "measure of the fish."[22] The same () is the symbol for the Holy Spirit in Christian iconography. Was this identity of Mary Magdalene the secret knowledge of the Gnostics? Their communities were harshly chastised in the second through fourth centuries for practicing "numbers theology." Since Jesus was called the *Ichthys*, "the Fish," is it not likely that the woman identified with the "measure of the fish" was perceived to be his partner? Because this coded information has been embedded in the Gospels themselves, the rumor of the intimacy of Christ and Mary Magdalene has resurfaced over and over during the Christian millennium. Virulent and irrepressible, like a sturdy vine, this old mythology spreads underground during periods of persecution and then resurfaces and thrives for awhile, as it did in the "Grail heresy" of thirteenth-century France and again in the twentieth century in popular works like *Jesus Christ, Superstar* and *Godspell*.

In the wake of the discovery of the Gnostic library at the Nag Hammadi site in the Egyptian desert, scholars are reexamining the identity and role of Mary Magdalene. Citing nearly two thousand years of Church tradition, some conservative Roman Catholic scholars insist that Mary Magdalene was from a town in Galilee now called Magdala, although this theory is not sustained by the grammatical ending of her epithet. Recent scholarship shows that the Magdalene was a favorite apostle of Jesus and carried the "Good

News" of his Resurrection to the male apostles who did not accompany her to the tomb on Easter morning. This interpretation of Mary's role gives her special status and equal authority with the male apostles and provides an appropriate model for nuns seeking ordination and equality with the male Roman Catholic clergy. For many, this proposed sharing of priestly power by religious women seems radical enough.

But does the proposed model reflect the whole truth? Was Mary Magdalene a mere apostle? Or was she, in fact, as the Gnostic Gospel of Philip suggests, the consort of Christ? If she was his intimate companion and "consort," and if their

The archetypal image of women praying together, as they have since they walked with Jesus in Palestine. These women are mid-twentieth-century pilgrims to the site of the apparitions of the Blessed Mother at Fatima in Portugal.

hieros gamos union was actually at the heart of the group that knew and honored them, then giving Magdalene the status of a disciple or even an apostle is clearly inadequate—a far cry from the exalted status she would claim as Bride of the sacrificed "Bridegroom of Israel." She would be the embodiment of the archetypal "Widow of Sion" who laments her sacrificed Bridegroom and the destruction of the Temple. The gematria encoded in passages of the Greek New Testament confirms the latter interpretation: that the partnership of Christ and Magdalene was indigenous to the Christian community.[23] The authors of the four canonical Gospels recognized them as the "Lord and Lady of the Fishes."

So strong is the Bride's suppressed energy that women worldwide have in recent decades been experiencing visions of Mary Magdalene and Jesus holding hands or sharing a warm embrace. How ironic that the same Church that deplores divorce on the basis of the words of Jesus recorded in the Gospels has managed to keep him separated from the woman with whom, according to the Gnostic Gospel of Philip, he shared a special intimacy, the woman Philip calls the "consort" of Jesus, whom he kissed often on the mouth. The image of their sacred reunion has healing in its wings, providing a true partnership model for Christianity that is soundly based in its own sacred texts. In the original foundation myth of Christianity, the Magdalene was not merely an apostle or disciple of the crucified Lord. She was his Beloved.

Perhaps it is time to reclaim the ancient model for wholeness and holiness found in the sacrificed Bridegroom and his forgotten counterpart and beloved, the lost Bride of the Christian story. Her gentle presence, her quiet strength, and her steadfast and passionate devotion for her Lord has long been a model for the devotion of the Church to her Savior. It is not equal power with the priests/apostles that she seeks; it is, quite simply, union with the Beloved. Her longing for Christ is the model for each ardent soul in its search for God. For Mary Magdalene and for the followers of the "Christian Way," it has been a long journey!

THE PRACTICE OF THE PRESENCE OF GOD

To facilitate the practice of the presence of God, it is suggested that you find an unusual ring and wear it as a reminder of your commitment to this practice. Or, if you already wear such a ring, switch it to the opposite hand to make yourself more conscious of its presence on your finger. If you do not own a ring, perhaps you could use strands of colorful embroidery thread to braid a ring for yourself. Every time you notice your ring, allow it to remind you to think of God present with you, in the secluded "chapel of your heart." You should remember to acknowledge your intimate companion on your faith journey. Whenever you notice the ring, pause and speak to God. Tell him whatever is on your mind: your thoughts, your fears, your aspirations. Speak to God as you would to a close friend or lover. Thank God for his many generous gifts to you and those you love, and ask him for things you need. Pour out your heart at God's feet, the way Mary poured her precious nard over the feet of Jesus. Gradually, over a period of days and weeks, you will find this practice becoming second nature, whether or not you notice the ring on your finger.

Suggested Liturgy for Advent

During Advent, the four-week period preceding Christmas, it is customary to prepare for the coming of the Divine Christ Child with simple acts of self-denial and liturgical prayers. Traditionally, an evergreen wreath is formed with four candles placed at even intervals. On each Sunday in Advent, a new candle is lit, so that, at the end of the period, all four are burned together, increasing the light as we near the birth of the "Light of the World" which occurs, appropriately, almost on the same date as the winter solstice, the time when the sun begins its return in the northern hemisphere.

Here we offer an alternative symbolic Advent decoration and liturgy, combining the masculine fire and feminine water symbols in a sacred union.

First, create a symbolic decoration. Select a crystal chalice or bowl and fill it with clear water. Float a small round tea candle, preferably one with a six-pointed star or flower design. The Spirit is present in the flame, floating on the waters of the sacred Chalice, representing our planet earth, the "water carrier," and also the heart of each human vessel. After a few minutes of silence, say a meaningful prayer of your own creation, or if you prefer, read this prayer:

Emmanuel

Come, O come, Emmanuel!
Come to dwell in our midst!
We long to be the community
where God dwells in each heart.

Fill us with a new consciousness
of balance and wholeness,
of the sacred marriage,
of male and female,
of fire and water,
of reason and love,
in our own hearts,
in all our relationships,
in all our thoughts and actions.

Make us aware of the danger
of fire without water,
for we have seen fearful holocausts.

Make us aware of the danger
of water without fire,
for we have seen the chaos
of irresponsible excesses.

Help us avoid selfish choices
of unbridled individualism and pleasure-seeking.
Teach us to be passionate custodians
of our planet,
Cherishing the bountiful gifts she bestows—
nourishment, peaceful harmony, and beauty.

And teach us to cherish each child of this mother
formed from the union of God and earth,
for there is but one Child.

We are Emmanuel,
the community that sees the face of God
in one another,
and in serving one another, serves God.

Notes

1. James Robinson, ed. "The Gospel of Philip." Translated by Wesley W. Isenberg in *The Nag Hammadi Library: In English*. San Francisco: Harper & Row, 1981, p.136. First published Leiden, The Netherlands: E.J. Brill, 1978.

2. Ibid., 472. From "The Gospel of Mary." Translated by George W. MacRae and R. McL. Wilson.

3. Ibid., 475–477, "The Act of Peter." Translated by James Brashler and Douglas M. Parrott.

4. Laura Swan, *The Forgotten Desert Mother: Sayings, Lives and Stories of Early Christian Women*. New York: Paulist Press, 2001, p.3. Sister Laura cites Palladius in *Lausaic History* for this estimate.

5. Ibid., p.88.

6. Ibid., pp.89–90.

7. Excerpt from "The Deer's Cry" (Saint Patrick) translated by Kuno Meyer from *Selections from Ancient Irish Poetry*, edited by Kuno Meyer. London: Constable & Co., Ltd., 1911.

8. Ibid.

9. "Be Thou My Vision," translated by Mary Byrne, 1927, from an ancient Irish hymn. Published in *The Armed Forces Hymnal*. Washington, D.C.: U.S. Government Printing Office.

10. Quote from *Hildegard Von Bingen's Mystical Visions: Translated from Scivias*. Translated by Bruce Hozeski. Santa Fe. N.M. Bear & Co., reprint edition 1995, p.77.

11. Excerpt from "Myrrh-Bearers" by Margaret Junkin Preston (d. 1897).

12. See Margaret Starbird, *The Goddess in the Gospels: Reclaiming the Sacred Feminine*. Santa Fe, N.M.: Bear & Company, 1998, Appendix iv, pp.159–60.

13. From "The Rosy Sequence" (Saint Bernard of Clairvaux?), translated by John Mason Neale (d. 1866).

14. Excerpt from "On Pope Innocent III" by Walther von der Vogelweide, translated by Jethro Bithell from *The Minnesingers*. London: Longmans, 1909.

15. Excerpt from "The Song of the Creatures" by Saint Francis of Assisi, tr. Matthew Arnold (d. 1888).

16. See Denis de Rougemont, *Love in the Western World*, translated by Montgomery Belgion. New York: Pantheon Books, 1956.

17. Joan Chittister, Sister, O.S.B., from her speech "Spirituality and Contemporary Culture II." The 2000 TCPC National Forum.

18. Neil Douglas-Klotz, *Prayers of the Cosmos: Meditations on the Aramaic Words of Jesus*. San Francisco: Harper & Row, 1990, p.12.

19. Ibid., p.34.

20. See William E. Phipps, *The Sexuality of Jesus*. Cleveland, Ohio: Pilgrim Press, 1996. Includes a detailed discussion of the possibility that Jesus was married.

21. Robinson, ed. "The Gospel of Philip," op. cit., p.138.

22. See Starbird, *The Goddess in the Gospels*, op.cit., pp.159–160, for further explanation of the New Testament gematria and sacred geometry connected with Mary Magdalene and the *Vesica Piscis*.

23. Ibid.

Chronology

B.C.E.	7–4	Birth of Jesus. The exact date cannot be established.
C.E.	28–29	Ministry of Jesus
	c. 29	Crucifixion of Jesus
	35	Conversion of Saul/Paul
	42	Mary Magdalene and her siblings and companions arrive in southern France (French legend)
	46–57	Paul's missionary journeys, Epistles
	70	Fall of Jerusalem to the Roman Army
	50–90	Christian Church of Saint Mary at Glastonbury (legend)
	c. 70	Gospel of Mark
	c. 80	Gospel of Matthew
	c. 85	Gospel of Luke
	c. 90	Gospel of John
	95–100	Book of Revelation
	44–325	Persecutions of Christians in the Roman Empire
	200–565	Desert ascetics, Abbas and Ammas
	150–300	Gnostic Gospels written
	250–400	Christian catacombs in crypt of Saint Victor in Marseilles
	325	Council of Nicea, Christianity accepted in the Roman Empire
	354–430	Saint Augustine of Hippo
	354–418	Pelagius, British/Irish theologian
	374–419	Saint Jerome (translated the Scriptures into Latin)
	380–460	Amma Syncletica, desert ascetic
	389–461	Saint Patrick
	400	Gnostic Gospels buried in jars at Nag Hammadi
	480–543	Saint Benedict of Nursia, the founder of the Benedictine order
	500–550	Maria the Harp-player, hermit ascetic
	500–1000	The Dark Ages in western Europe
	d. 524	Saint Brigid
	521–597	Saint Columba, Irish missionary to the continent
	663	Synod of Whitby, Hilda of Whitby presiding
	675–754	Saint Boniface, Irish missionary to Germanic tribes
	732–804	Alcuin, scholar-theologian, Charlemagne's advisor
	800	Charlemagne crowned Holy Roman Emperor by Pope Leo
	935–999	Hrotswitha of Gandersheim, nun, playwright
	1000–1500	The Middle Ages in Europe
	1090–1153	Saint Bernard of Clairvaux
	1098–1099	First Crusade conquers Jerusalem
	1098–1179	Hildegard of Bingen
	1100–1250	Building of the great French cathedral of "Notre Dame"
	1181–1226	Saint Francis of Assisi
	1194–1253	Saint Clare
	1210–1285	Mechtild of Magdeburg
	1209–1255	Albigensian Crusade against Cathars in southern France
	1244	Fall of Montségur, Cathar stronghold
	1347–1380	Saint Catherine of Siena
	1412–1431	Joan of Arc, "Maid of Orléans" leads French armies
	1483–1546	Martin Luther, leader of Protestant Reformation
	1515–1582	Saint Teresa of Avila, Spanish Carmelite nun, mystic
	1614–1691	Brother Lawrence (Nicholas Herman), mystic
	1873–1897	Saint Thérèse of Lisieux, "The Little Flower of Jesus"
	1858	Bernadette Soubirous receives vision at Lourdes
	1914–1918	First World War
	1917	Visions of "Our Lady of Fatima"
	1910–1997	Mother Teresa of Calcutta
	1939–1945	Second World War
	1981	First apparition of Our Lady at Medjugorje

Glossary

Albigensian Crusade—war waged by several popes and French kings against heretics in southern France, especially Cathars, from 1209–1250.

Albigensian heresy—medieval heresy prevalent in southern France characterized as dualistic and anticlerical.

Anawim—the little ones, or indigenous "poor" and disenfranchised people of God.

Apocalypse—The final book of the canonical New Testament, the Book of Revelation.

Aramaic—language spoken by native peoples in Palestine/Israel during the time of Jesus.

Archetype—model or pattern of human experience universally recognized: mother, warrior, divine child, sage.

Assisi—town in Tuscany, home of Saint Francis.

Bogomils—Balkan Christians participating in a populist reformation of Christianity, thought to be the forebears of the Cathar/Albigensian heresy.

Canon—the officially accepted books of Scripture; the canonical New Testament.

Cathar Heresy—dualist heresy related to Manichaeism, probably derived from faith and tenets of Bogomils.

Chaplet—rosary with beads for only one decade with several introductory beads.

Chartres Cathedral—twelfth to thirteenth-century cathedral of Our Lady just south of Paris.

Eucharist—shared meal of thanksgiving; the sacrament of Holy Communion.

Evangelist—author of a Gospel or person who preaches the Gospel.

Franciscans—friars who were followers of Saint Francis of Assisi.

Gnostic Christianity—early sect encouraged "knowing" God through personal enlightenment rather than "organized"/mandatory sacraments, rituals, and prayers.

Gnostic Gospels—written texts of Gnostic Christians hidden in earthen jars in the Egyptian desert during period of persecution by the orthodox (c. 400).

Golgotha—hill outside Jerusalem where Jesus was said to have been crucified by Roman soldiers.

Gospel—the "Good News" of salvation through the life, death, and Resurrection of Jesus (see also Gnostic Gospels).

Hellenized—heavily influenced by classical Greek culture and philosophy.

Hieros Gamos—the "Sacred Marriage" of the masculine and feminine energies celebrated in fertility rites in ancient cults indigenous to the Near East.

Holy Grail—Sacred chalice, symbolic of the Sacred Feminine and the subject of medieval romance and myth.

Inquisition—Judicial body instituted by the Roman Catholic pope in 1237 to investigate heresy and to judge and execute heretics.

Isis—Egyptian goddess, "Queen of Heaven and Earth," consort of the sun god Osiris.

Jerusalem—the Holy City in Israel, symbolic Daughter of Sion and Bride of God.

Kerygma—the promises inherent in the life, death, and Resurrection of Jesus Christ—the "Good News" of salvation.

Koiné **Greek**—the "lingua franca" or common language of the Middle East in the early centuries of Christianity.

Koinonos—Greek for "intimate companion, consort," used in the Gospel of Philip to describe Mary Magdalene, the "consort" of the Savior.

Labyrinth—spiral path that provides a metaphor for the soul's sacred journey, often used as a meditation tool.

Madonna—sculpture or icon/painting of the Mother of Jesus, Our Lady, or Feminine aspect of the Divine.

Manna—food that fed the Hebrews in the desert in a miraculous fashion (Book of Exodus), symbolic of the bread of God, the Christian Eucharist.

Messiah—Hebrew word for the "anointed one" and the "Bridegroom of Israel." The promised Messiah was to be from the royal lineage of King David.

Nag Hammadi—site in Egypt where the Gnostic codices (fourth-century sacred texts) were discovered buried in jars.

New Testament—the Christian canon written in Greek; the compilation of four Gospels, numerous epistles of Paul and other early Christian leaders, and the Books of Acts and Revelation. Translated into Latin by Jerome (4th century).

Parable—metaphorical story using homely images to teach a philosophical or ethical truth.

Pater Noster—Latin title for the "Lord's Prayer."

Parousia—the promise of the immediate return of Jesus Christ and the advent of the Kingdom of God; reconciliation of heaven and earth through divine intervention.

Reformation—movement of religious free thinkers who worked to reform the medieval Roman Catholic Church. Great leaders include Martin Luther, John Calvin, John Wyclife, Sir Thomas More, John Wesley.

Rosary—circle of beads divided into decades upon which specific prayers are said to Our Lady Mary, the mother of Jesus. Praying with a rosary often encourages altered consciousness and is used in ancient goddess cults and other religions for supplication and meditation.

Sacrament—an outward sign of grace usually dispensed by Christian minister or priest.

Saint—an officially acknowledged friend, follower, or disciple of Jesus canonized by the Roman Catholic Church.

Sophia—Holy Wisdom, the Greek personification of the Holy Spirit, the "consort" or "mirror" of God.

Taizé—Ecumenical retreat and charismatic renewal center in France.

Theotokos—"God-bearer"; epithet of the Virgin Mary, "Mother of God."

Trinity, Holy—the threefold aspects of the Godhead: Father, Son, and Holy Spirit.

Vesica Piscis—the "Vessel of the Fish"—formed when two equal circles intersect through their centers. It was known as the *matrix* of all other geometric shapes and is an ancient symbol for the feminine and the goddess. It was adopted into Christianity as a symbol for the Holy Spirit and the Sophia.

Suggested Reading

Aradi, Zsolt. *Shrines of Our Lady Around the World*. New York: Farrar, Straus & Young, 1954.

Artress, Lauren. *Walking a Sacred Path: Rediscovering the Labyrinth as a Spiritual Tool*. New York: Putnam Publishing Group, 1995.

Armstrong, Regis J., and I.C. Brady, eds. *Francis and Clare: Complete Works*. New York: Paulist Press, 1982.

Auclair, Marcelle. *Saint Teresa of Avila*. Petersham, Mass.: St Bede's Publications, 1988.

Barclay, James. *The Mind of Jesus*. New York: Harper & Row, 1960.

Beben, Mary. *New Wine*. Boulder, Colo.: WovenWord Press, 2002.

Bayley, Harold. *The Lost Language of Symbolism*. Totowa, N.J.: Rowman & Littlefield, 1974. First published 1912.

Begg, Ian. *The Cult of the Black Virgin*. New York: Penguin Books, 1985.

Bodo, Murray O. *A Light in the Garden*. Cincinnati: St. Anthony Messenger Press, 1992.

Bodo, Murray O., and Susan Saint Sing. *Francis & Clare of Assisi: Following Our Pilgrim Hearts*. Cincinnati: Anthony Messenger Press, 1986.

Boom, Corrie ten. *The Hiding Place*. Uhrichsville, Ohio: Barbour & Co., 1984.

Boom, Corrie ten. *Tramp for the Lord*. New York: Jove Publications, 1984.

Bongie, Elizabeth Bryan, trans. *The Life of Blessed Syncletica by Pseudo-Athanasius*. Toronto: Peregrina Publishing, 1995.

Brunn, Emilie Zum, and Georgette Epiney-Burgard. *Women Mystics in Medieval Europe*. New York: Paragon House, 1989.

Cartlidge, David R., and David L. Dungan. *Documents for Study of the Gospels*. Philadelphia: Fortress Press, 1980.

Curry, Dayna, Heather Mercer, and Stacy Mattingly. *Prisoners of Hope: The Story of Our Captivity and Freedom in Afghanistan*. New York: Doubleday, 2002.

Curry, Helen, and Jean Houston. *The Way of the Labyrinth: A Powerful Meditation for Everyday Life*. New York: Penguin USA, 2000.

Di Monte, Ugolino, ed. *The Little Flowers of St. Francis of Assisi* (Vintage Spiritual Classics). New York: Vintage Books, reprinted 1998.

Durkin Dierks, Sheila. *Woman Eucharist*. Boulder, Colo.: Woven Word Press, 1997.

Douglas-Klotz, Neil. *Prayers of the Cosmos: Meditations on the Aramaic Words of Jesus*. San Francisco: Harper & Row, 1990.

Douglas-Klotz, Neil. *The Hidden Gospel: Decoding the Spiritual Message of the Aramaic Jesus*. Wheaton, Ill.: Quest Books, 1999.

Englebert, Omer. *Saint Francis of Assisi: A Biography*. Ann Arbor, Mich.: Servant Publications, 1982.

Fideler, David. *Jesus Christ, Sun of God*. Wheaton, Ill.: Quest Books, 1993.

Fiorenza, Elisabeth Schüssler. *In Memory of Her*. New York: Crossroads, 1988.

Flinders, Carol Lee. *Enduring Grace: Living Portraits of Seven Women Mystics*. San Francisco: Harper & Row, 1993.

Fox, Matthew. *Original Blessing*. Santa Fe, N. Mexico: Bear and Co., 1988.

Flanagan, Sabina. *Hildegard of Bingen, 1098–1179: A Visionary Life*. London: Routledge, 1998.

Funk, Robert L., ed., with Roy W. Hoover and the Jesus Seminar. *The Five Gospels*. New York: The Macmillan Publishing Co., 1993.

Galvani, Christiane Mesch, trans. *Mechtild von Magdeburg, Flowing Light of the Divinity*. New York: Garland Publishing, 1991.

Goldin, Frederick, trans. *Lyrics of the Troubadours and Trouvères*. Garden City, N.Y.: Anchor Books, Doubleday & Co., 1973.

Green, Julien, and Peter Heinegg. *God's Fool: The Life and Times of Francis of Assisi*. San Francisco: Harper & Row, 1987.

Halliday, W.R. *The Pagan Background of Early Christianity*. New York: Cooper Square Publishers, 1970.

Haskins, Susan. *Mary Magdalen: Myth and Metaphor*. New York: Harcourt, Brace & Co., 1993.

Hozeski, Bruce, trans. *Hildegard Von Bingen's Mystical Visions: Translated from Scivias*. Santa Fe, N.M.: Bear and Co., reprint edition 1995.

Hulme, F. Edward. *Symbolism in Christian Art*. London: Swan, Sonnenschein & Co., 1891. Reprinted Detroit: Gale Research Co.,1969.

Jones, Charles W., ed. *Medieval Literature in Translation*. New York: Longmans, Green and Co., 1950.

Kramer, Samuel Noah. *The Sacred Marriage Rite*. Bloomington, Ind.: Indiana University Press, 1969.

Lawrence, Brother. *The Practice of the Presence of God*. Translated by John J. Delaney. New York: Doubleday, 1977.

Leloup, Jean-Yves, trans. from Coptic. *The Gospel of Mary Magdalene*. Translated into English and notes by Joseph Rowe. Vermont: Inner Traditions International, Bear & Co., 2002.

Leonhardt, Tom. *Giving Thanks with the Aramaic Jesus*. Boulder, Colo.: WovenWord Press, 2002.

Malvern, Marjorie. *Venus in Sackcloth*. Edwardsville, Ill.: Southern Illinois University Press, 1975.

Muggeridge, Malcolm. *Something Beautiful for God: Mother Teresa of Calcutta*. San Francisco: Harper & Row, 1986.

Newman, Barbara, ed. *Voice of the Living Light: Hildegard of Bingen and Her World*. Berkeley, Calif.: University of California Press, 1998.

O'Connor, Patricia. *Thérèse of Lisieux: A Biography*. Huntington, Ind.: Our Sunday Visitor, 1984.

O'Donohue, John. *Anam Cara: A Book of Celtic Wisdom*. New York: HarperCollins, 1997.

O'Mahoney, Christopher. *St. Thérèse of Lisieux by Those Who Knew Her*. San Francisco: Ignatius Press, 1989.

Oldenbourg, Zoé. *Massacre at Montségur*. Translated by Peter Green. New York: Pantheon Books, 1961.

Pagels, Elaine. *The Gnostic Gospels*. New York: Vintage Books, 1981.

Phipps, William E. *The Sexuality of Jesus*. Cleveland, Ohio: Pilgrim Press, 1996.

Piat, Stephane-Joseph, O.F.M. *Céline: Sister and Witness to St. Thérèse of the Child Jesu*. San Francisco: Ignatius Press, 1997.

Ranke-Heinemann, Ute. *Eunuchs for the Kingdom of Heaven*. Garden City, N.J: Doubleday, 1990.

Raymond of Capua. *The Life of St. Catherine of Siena*. Translated by George Lamb. Chicago: P.J. Kennedy & Sons, 1960.

Robinson, James M., ed. *The Nag Hammadi Library: In English*. New York: Harper & Row, 1981. First Published Leiden, The Netherlands: E.J. Brill, 1978.

Rougemont, Denis de. *Love in the Western World*. Translated by Montgomery Belgion. New York: Pantheon Books, 1956.

Spink, Kathryn. *A Universal Heart: The Life and Vision of Brother Roger of Taizé*. New York: HarperCollins, 1987.

Starbird, Margaret. *The Woman with the Alabaster Jar: Mary Magdalen and the Holy Grail*. Santa Fe, N.M.: Bear & Co., 1993.

Starbird, Margaret. *Magdalene's Lost Legacy*. Inner Traditions International, Bear and Company., 2003.

Swan, Laura. O.S.B. *The Forgotten Desert Mothers*. New York: Paulist Press, 2001.

Teresa of Calcutta, Mother. *A Simple Path*. New York: Ballantine Books, 1995.

Thérèse of Lisieux. *The Story of a Soul*: The Autobiography of St. Thérèse of Lisieux. Trans. John Clarke, O.C.D. Washington, D.C.: Institute of Carmelite Studies, 1972.

Torjesen, Karen Jo. *When Women Were Priests: Women's Leadership in the Early Church and the Scandal of Their Subordination in the Rise of Christianity*. New York: HarperCollins, 1993.

Ward, Benedicta. *The Sayings of the Desert Fathers*. Kalamazoo, Mich.: Cistercian Publications, 1975.

Woodruff, Sue. *Meditations With Mechtild of Magdeburg*. Santa Fe, N.M.: Bear and Co., 1982.

Warner, Marina. *Alone of All Her Sex: The Myth and the Cult of the Virgin Mary*. New York: Alfred A. Knopf. 1976. First published London: Weidenfeld & Nicolson, 1976.

Bibles

Holy Bible: New International Version. New York: The National Bible Society, 1978.

Saint Joseph New Catholic Edition of the Holy Bible. New York: Catholic Book Publishing Co., 1963.

Index

Acknowledgments

Bridgewater Books would like to thank the following for the permission to reproduce copyright material:
Bridgeman Art Library: pp. 69 Private Collection: 78 Stadelsches Kunstinstitut, Frankfurt-am-Main.
Bridgewater Book Co. Library: p. 23. Corbis: pp. 2, 4, 6, 11, 12, 13, 14, 18, 20, 25, 26, 31, 32, 36, 38, 43,
53, 59, 61, 66, 70, 75, 76, 77, 81, 83, 87, 89, 90, 93, 94, 99, 102, 103, 104, 106, 108, 111, 112, 117.
Sarah Howerd: p. 88. Gerard Hutton: p. 65. Image Bank: p. 57. GettyOneStone: pp: 41. Telegraph Colour
Library: p. 85. Cover: Main picture: Corbis. Inset: Bridgeman Art Library, St. Margaret's Church, Rottingdean.

Margaret Starbird would like to thank Mary T. Beben for the inspiration behind the "Emmanuel" Advent
decoration and Annette Hulefield for permission to share her Marian dreams.